W9-BXQ-150

to Innovation Park
and (80) (220) (322)

Innovation Park at Penn State

Distance	0.25 mile
Walking Time	4-5 minutes

PENN STATE

University
Park
1855

THIS IS PENN STATE

THIS IS

PENN STATE

An Insider's Guide to the University Park Campus

THE PENNSYLVANIA STATE UNIVERSITY PRESS

UNIVERSITY PARK, PENNSYLVANIA

A KEYSTONE BOOK™

A Keystone Book is so designated to distinguish it from the typical scholarly monograph that a university press publishes. It is a book intended to serve the citizens of Pennsylvania by educating them and others, in an entertaining way, about aspects of the history, culture, society, and environment of the state as part of the Middle Atlantic region.

LIBRARY OF CONGRESS CATALOGING-IN-PUBLICATION DATA

This is Penn State : an insider's guide to the University Park Campus.
      p.   cm.
  Includes bibliographical references and index.
  ISBN 0-271-02720-7 (pbk. : alk. paper)
  1. Pennsylvania State University—Guidebooks.
  2. Pennsylvania State University—Buildings—Guidebooks.
  I. Pennsylvania State University.

  LD4481.P83T52 2005
  378.748'53—dc22
  2005014672

THE PENNSYLVANIA STATE UNIVERSITY PRESS is a member of the Association of American University Presses.

It is the policy of The Pennsylvania State University Press to use acid-free paper. Publications on uncoated stock satisfy the minimum requirements of American National Standard for Information Sciences—Permanence of Paper for Printed Library Material, ANSI Z39.48–1992.

For the glory of old State

For her founders strong and great

For the future that we wait

CONTENTS

WHAT ENDURES: THE LANDSCAPE AT UNIVERSITY PARK   105

GABRIEL WELSCH

EAST CAMPUS

I'll admit, when Penn State Press asked me to write the foreword for this book, I had mixed feelings. Sure, I'm qualified for the job: I was born in 1855, the same year Penn State was founded, and in the three decades I worked for the school, I did everything from hauling the limestone used to build the first Old Main to acting as Penn State's mascot (long before anybody had ever heard of a Nittany Lion—whatever *that* is). Yes, on the one hand, I seemed like the perfect choice. But on the other hand, I've been dead for 112 years. Which was, well, kind of a strike against. Nowadays, I'm nothing but some bones held together by metal pins. I spend all of my time in a glass display case. And even when I was alive . . . I was a mule. Why would I write a foreword? Still, they kept asking. "Help us out, Old Coaly," they said. "No," I said. *"Please?"* they said. "Quit getting your fingerprints all over my display case," I said. "Why don't you go annoy Coach Paterno for a while?" I added.

But the folks at the Press kept at it, and when people are that dedicated and insistent, it's hard to just walk away. (Especially when you don't have any muscle tissue or tendons to move your leg bones.) So I finally broke down and read the book. And believe it or not, it's actually pretty good. It certainly doesn't address every single location on campus—try to find even one reference to the old veterinary hospital, a building so important that I was once stored in its atttic. And what about the Horse Barn? Where's the probing architectural analysis? But then again, I guess this book isn't supposed to be comprehensive. It's a guidebook that focuses on a few highlights of the University Park campus—past, present, and future. (At least that's what they told me. "Then where's the Salvage Warehouse?" I said.)

The volume in your hands is a valuable contribution to the growing body of Penn State Insider's Guide literature. And I know a thing or two about value: in 1863, the Farmers' High School bought me for $198. Adjusting for inflation, that's somewhere around $3,000, or roughly the cost of an intro-level speech-com textbook. Seriously, what's that paper made of, recycled diamonds? How much could it possibly cost to reprint that "Checkers" speech *again?* Anyway, sorry—what was I talking about?

Buy this book and enjoy it. It's useful, informative, and entertaining. I guarantee that there's no other book currently available that will show you the location of Old Botany, teach you the history of the Burrowes Fraternities, *and* finally reveal all the gritty details of what went on inside that box of mystery, the Calorimeter. (I know, but I'm not telling. Buy the book if you want to find out. I don't get royalties if you don't spend money. And if you think mule-skeleton polish is cheap, think again.)

OLD COALY

A Glass Case,
HUB–Robeson Center
University Park

PREFACE

As the University's sesquicentennial and Penn State Press's fiftieth anniversary approached, the staff at the Press (proud alumni among us) felt inspiration strike. Why not publish a book in honor of the University—our parent institution—and celebrate both milestones?

Options were weighed. Some of us suggested an almanac or an updated history of the University. Others preferred a richly illustrated volume that would put Penn Staters' coffee tables to good use. But ultimately we decided that a practical guidebook to the University Park campus, one replete with photos and historical anecdotes, would not only recognize the University's history but also offer a tour of the campus to new generations of the Penn State family.

We knew that the campus architecture would tell a compelling story about the University's growth. But we hoped for more than that. Our guide would certainly offer a tour of notable buildings, but we also wanted it to spotlight some of the milestones of the University's first 150 years and to relate personal stories from alumni and others who make Penn State a living institution.

Penn State librarian Leon J. Stout graciously guided us as we narrowed our list of noteworthy buildings—a difficult task, of course, because *every* building has a story worth telling. We invited alumni to share their recollections of Penn State with us. And we began our research in earnest, poring over documents and photographs in the University Archives, marveling over changes to the campus and little-known pieces of the Penn State story.

Who could have imagined that the entire population—students, faculty, and administrators—of the Farmers' High School, as Penn State was known in 1855, originally lived, studied, ate, and slept in one building? That the new Information Sciences and Technology Building was modeled after a fourteenth-century Italian bridge? That the Pavilion Theatre was designed for judging livestock? That Old Coaly, a hardworking mule from the earliest days of the school, was so popular that the students embraced him as their informal mascot—long before the Nittany Lion? And who could have guessed that the innumerable brazen squirrels on campus could be traced back to just four pairs of furry rodents?

These and other fascinating discoveries await you in our "insider's guide" to Penn State. Enjoy your tour of the University Park campus. We hope that you will return again and again!

We gratefully acknowledge the people who helped make this book a reality. Sandy Thatcher, director of Penn State Press, threw his complete support behind the project early on. Many thanks go to Leon J. Stout, Craig Zabel, and Gabriel Welsch, as well as all of those alumni who shared their tales of "dear old State"; the members of the University's Sesquicentennial Committee, Steve MacCarthy, Mike Bezilla, Jackie Esposito, Patricia Farrell, Roni Francke, Charlene A. Friedman, Charlene Harrison, Linda Higginson, Kay Kustanbauter, Eston Martz, Barb Meeker, Lisa Powers, and Jim Purdum; the staff of the University Archives, as well as Bonnie McEwan, Catherine Grigor, and Wilson Hutton at the University Libraries; the Office of Public Information, particularly Chris Koleno and Bill Mahon; and Erin Greb and the Gould Center. Special thanks to Greg Grieco whose generosity of time and many photographs truly made this book possible. Stopping by the office to check on the schedule didn't hurt, either.

We appreciate the help of the Alumni Association, especially Roger Williams and Tina Hay; Therese D. Boyd and Joseph G. Pizarchik (Class of '79); Davin Carr-Chellman and Mya Pawlicki at the Center for Ethics and Religious Affairs; Donna Merrill and Steve Watson at the College of Agricultural Sciences; Paul Kletchka and Amy Marshall at the College of Arts and Architecture; Danna Smith and Diana Wagner at the College of Engineering; S. William Hessert Jr. at the College of Health and Human Development; the *Daily Collegian*; Mike Fleck at the Department of Materials Science and Engineering; Krista Kahler at the Frost Entomological Museum; IKM Incorporated; the Mitchell and Campbell families; Randy Thompson at Phi Delta Theta; Joyce Robinson; Steve Sampsell; Tomas W. Schaller; Gwynne D. Kinley at the Schreyer Honors College; Ginger Breon, Ian Nalepa, and Brian Barton at the Smeal College of Business Administration; Jennifer Smith; Bob Corman and Joy Sinclair at Telecommunications and Networking Services; Cathy Stout at University Health Services; Jeffrey T. Herman at University Publications; *La Vie*; Steve Walton; and Devon Zahn.

Entire buildings were erected on campus in the time it took us to write, edit, and produce this book. Then they moved the Creamery, and we had to start over. The book was underway before some of us started working at PSU, and it was still underway as others left for new ventures. Our thanks to those who took part in the drudgery but missed the book's release: Anne Davis, for her research and copywriting, and Stephanie Grace ("Sesqui Hanna"), for tracking down photos and decoding acronyms. Thanks especially to former editor-in-chief Peter Potter, who had the discipline to set rigid deadlines and the decency to extend them a dozen times. He kept the project alive when despairing seemed easier than making another trip to the Archives. We appreciate it.

WITH THANKS

PENN STATE'S UNIVERSITY PARK CAMPUS
ITS EVOLUTION AND GROWTH

LEON J. STOUT

Today's University Park campus is often seen as the quintessential university campus by visitors and Penn State loyalists alike. The diversity and near-urban concentration of buildings are balanced by manicured lawns with magnificent stands of trees, shrubs, and flowers. The contrast between the present campus and what the first students would have seen on their arrival in 1859—an unfinished building and rough grounds littered with rocks and tree stumps—could not be more dramatic. Yet when Governor James Pollock signed the charter for the new institution on February 22, 1855, its trustees had no idea where it would even be located, let alone what it would teach its future students. Penn State in its early days was a pioneer school in many ways but always seemed to be playing catch-up when it came to a physical plant to meet its needs. It was a school that was literally invented from the ground up, and this is the story of its central campus.

THE EARLY COLLEGE BUILDINGS

One of the most significant questions facing the trustees of the infant Farmers' High School of Pennsylvania was where to establish the school. During the summer of 1855, they mulled over offers of land from Erie, Blair, Perry, Allegheny, Franklin, Dauphin, and Huntingdon Counties before settling on General James Irvin's offer of two hundred acres of land in Centre County. At the September 12, 1855, meeting of the trustees, Irvin offered an additional adjacent two hundred acres for purchase at a favorable price, and the citizens of the county offered a further donation of $10,000 to the new school to help it with the expenses of constructing a college building. The board eventually voted to accept the Centre County offer.

A number of factors influenced the selection of the Centre County site. Not the least of them was the prominence of those supporting the offer—

I would like to acknowledge the assistance of university architects David Zehngut and Silvi Lawrence, Professor Eliza Pennypacker of the Department of Landscape Architecture, and University historian Michael Bezilla in reviewing this essay and providing valuable suggestions.

General Irvin, Andrew Gregg Curtin, and Hugh Nelson McAllister. Irvin had served in Congress and been a candidate for governor. Curtin was Secretary of the Commonwealth and would be elected governor in 1861, while McAllister was a prominent Bellefonte attorney and officer of the state agricultural society. The county's central geographic location also played a role in its selection, although its isolation was probably more important. One farmer noted approvingly that students were "entirely out of the reach and influence of those temptations to vice and idleness, so common in and close around our cities and large towns." Another advantage was the site's location in the Nittany Valley, the state's second largest limestone valley with soils of outstanding fertility. The lack of surface water on the acreage did appear to be a problem in the early days; the water resources of the valley still represent a concern, although the problem is framed differently today. (Availability of water is not just a farm irrigation issue. We now understand that the whole Spring Creek watershed is one interconnected resource that is vital to the environmental, social, and economic needs of the entire valley.)

The original Old Main, still under construction, in 1859

The four hundred acres acquired from General Irvin had been mostly stripped of trees to make charcoal to power Centre Furnace, the first of Centre County's eight iron furnaces and only the second built west of the Susquehanna (in 1792). There were still two woodlots on the land that would become the campus—

Hort Woods, located north of today's arts buildings, and the remnant forest surrounding the Nittany Lion Inn. But the plot still required much work to make it suitable for farming. There were no existing structures on the land, nor was there anything more than an inn and a house or two across the road that would become College Avenue. The early student labor projects (requiring three hours a day from each student) went to readying the land, then plowing and planting. This all took place around a small cluster of buildings.

The College Building (usually referred to today as the original Old Main) was designed by Hugh McAllister, the Bellefonte lawyer who had become a local trustee. The massive five-story, five-bay structure was constructed of limestone quarried just a few hundred yards away. It was built on a rise facing a large open field—initially planted in farm crops, but later in grass—with the main road from Bellefonte to Spruce Creek at the foot of the rise. This arrangement, and in fact the look and functionality of the building, followed the model of Princeton's Nassau Hall, America's most imitated college building. For the students of the time, it *was* the college. It housed all: student rooms and faculty apartments, cooking and eating facilities, classrooms, laboratories, the library and museums, literary society rooms, and the president's office.

Lying behind the College Building to the west, where Carnegie Building stands today, were the College Barn and its small auxiliary structures. To the east was the residence of William G. Waring, horticulture professor and general administrative superintendent before the arrival of President Evan Pugh in 1859. Both the barn and Waring's house (later known as Oak Cottage) were in place by 1858. Construction on the College Building had begun in 1857, but that autumn's short-lived yet sharp financial panic kept donors from fulfilling their monetary pledges, and the contractors went bankrupt. It was only partially completed when the first students arrived in February 1859. (The College Building was not the "main" building until the late 1880s, and only became known as "Old Main" after 1900.) Evan Pugh, arriving on campus that October, invigorated the new school and by 1861, the trustees were ready to restart construction. With delays and material shortages caused by the Civil War, however, the building was not completed until December 1863.

In the following year, President Pugh laid out the design for a country Georgian president's residence, one with a central staircase, symmetrically flanking rooms, and an all-important library. He contributed half of the funds and construction began in the spring of 1864. Sadly, he would never live in the house; he died unexpectedly in April 1864. But in addition to the construction of the president's home, he had accomplished a vital task for the school. Thanks to Pugh's tireless lobbying, the Agricultural College of Pennsylvania (as the Farmers' High School was renamed in 1862) was designated Pennsylvania's land-grant college by the state legislature. While the benefits of the land-grant endowment were slow in coming to the College, the state's formal pledge of continuing support was vital to Penn State's future success.

THE ATHERTON ADMINISTRATION'S NEW BUILDINGS

With one additional residence—a house for the College's vice president, built in 1880—the campus would be complete until the first major building program

The gates at College Avenue and Allen Street in 1896

was initiated under Penn State's seventh president, George W. Atherton. The Pennsylvania State College (renamed in 1874) had struggled during the seventeen years following Pugh's death. When Atherton arrived in 1882, there were only eighty-seven students and there had rarely been more than a half-dozen degrees awarded in any year. Two recent legislative investigations had highlighted the College's curricular disarray and financial woes. But within six years, Atherton had refocused the College. He lobbied Congress for the passage of the Hatch Act in 1887, which created America's system of agricultural experiment stations and brought federal aid to land-grant colleges. He secured the first regular biennial state appropriation for Penn State as well as a series of appropriations to construct new buildings to support its future growth.

The Board of Trustees designated Frederick L. Olds as College Architect to design and help identify sites for these new buildings. Olds brought elements of Henry Hobson Richardson's Romanesque revival style and Frank Furness's Victorian eclecticism into six college buildings and six faculty residences built on campus between 1886 and 1893. The most significant of these was the Engineering Building, located at the corner of College Avenue and Allen Street—the site of today's Sackett Building. Old Engineering was a massive structure with a great arched entrance, onion-domed roofs on bartizans, and other dramatic ornamentation. It firmly established the campus location for engineering for the next century.

Perpendicular to Allen Street was a lane behind Old Main, now Pollock Road, where a number of the new structures were situated. The Armory was placed at the southwest corner of Allen Street and the road. It served the College as both a gymnasium and the home for military instruction, which was required by the Morrill Land-Grant Act. Diagonally across from it was the Old

Botany Building, now the home of the Science, Technology, and Society Program. Slightly behind that was the Ladies' Cottage, the first women's dormitory (razed in 1971). Farther east along both sides of the lane were placed the Chemistry and Physics Building and five faculty residences. A parallel road farther north up the hill became a location for additional residences, and to the east it bisected "Ag Hill," the location of the Agricultural Experiment Station building and barns. Between Ag Hill and the residences lay a grandstand and fields for football, baseball, and track—the "Old Beaver Field" area, which today is the parking lot behind Osmond Lab. While women now had a dormitory, male students still lived in Old Main, and, after 1887, in fraternity houses in town.

Chemistry and Physics Building, faculty residences, and McAllister Hall

The campus roads thus began to take on a grid alignment, while buildings set generously back from these roads gave the appearance of an academic village. A further sign of a campus plan was the initial placement of functional groupings of buildings for the disciplines of engineering, science, and agriculture in specific locations on the campus. In addition, these new buildings, with their modern architectural styles, began to provide a consistent appearance to the campus, in contrast to the older styles of Old Main and the president's house.

A second building program in the Atherton administration followed between 1899 and 1906 with new architects. It included the design and construction of Schwab Auditorium, Carnegie Library, McAllister Hall, the Armsby Building, and several wood-frame structures for forestry, mining, and dairy husbandry as well as additional faculty residences. The agriculture-related buildings expanded the Ag Hill group, and the auditorium, library, and McAllister (then a dormitory) were built around the back of Old Main, preserving the campus lawn in front. Some of the buildings and residences, however, were scattered over the property, giving a more casual appearance to the placement of buildings. Schwab, Carnegie, and McAllister were the first buildings designed in the new classical revival styles made popular by the 1893 World's Columbian Exposition in Chicago. Carnegie and McAllister were designed by Paul and Seymour Davis; Edward Hazlehurst was the architect for Schwab and Armsby. Hazlehurst termed his work "English Renaissance Revival," although it shared some design elements with the Richardson- and Furness-inspired buildings.

THE FIRST CAMPUS PLANS AND THE SPARKS ADMINISTRATION

Perhaps recognizing the seemingly haphazard growth that had occurred over the fifty previous years, the Board of Trustees commissioned the first campus plan in 1907. New York landscape architect Charles Lowrie took the existing layout and overlaid it with a more developed rectangular grid of streets, supplemented by diagonal avenues, and a number of new buildings that further expanded the disciplinary groupings. Under this plan, Allen Street would have become the primary north-south axis, and a central quad of arts and sciences buildings would rise to the north of the library. Surrounding this central group, in clockwise order, would have been groupings for engineering, fraternities, men's dorms, athletics, agriculture, women's dorms, faculty homes, and the president's residence (relocated to the location of today's Health and Human Development East Building). This zoned organization reflects the influence of the "Beaux-Arts Campus," the adaptation of monumental organizing schemes for cities first presented in the 1893 Chicago exposition's "White City."

Unfortunately, the Lowrie plan was delivered at a time of turmoil for the campus. President Atherton had died in 1906 and it took two years to find a new president. In the interim, General James A. Beaver, as Board of Trustees president, served as acting president of the College; deans, administrators, faculty, and students battled one another over direction and control. With the arrival of a new president, Edwin Erle Sparks, in 1908, a new campus architect—Charles Z. Klauder of the Philadelphia firm of Day and Klauder— came to develop a new master plan for the campus.

Klauder's first plan in 1914 changed the Lowrie concept by reducing the number of roads and paths on the campus and by creating more symmetrical quadrangles for the building groups that related more consistently to Old Main and its lawn as a focal point, rather than to Allen Street. Over the next twenty-five years, Klauder would design some of Penn State's most distinguished

buildings and continue developing the campus plan that would result in memorable spaces like the Pattee Mall and the West Halls Quad.

Financial constraints in the Sparks administration (1908–20) curbed construction, although Sparks began the first land expansion to the east, adding more than six hundred acres to the original four hundred. On campus, several new buildings were constructed on Ag Hill, along with the first phases of Pond Lab, the Sparks Building, and the Mining Building. Several other buildings received additions, and Engineering Units D and E were constructed. In November 1918, a terrible fire gutted Old Engineering, and in the next years, Engineering Units A, B, and C, as well as Reber Building, were built extending to the west of the Old Engineering site to fill the gap.

World War I brought traumatic changes to The Pennsylvania State College. New building construction was halted, and the Army virtually took over the College by inducting all male students into the Student Army Training

Returning from chapel along the path to Ag Hill

Corps. After the war, Dr. Sparks retired from the presidency. In the postwar period, veterans as well as increasing numbers of high school students wanted to attend Penn State. Enrollment topped three thousand, and applications may have been double that number. The trustees knew that they needed more buildings for "student welfare"—dormitories, a hospital, a student union, and gymnasiums.

The board hired a new president in 1921 with proven experience in fund-raising: John Martin Thomas. At the board's direction, Thomas planned the Two Million Dollar Emergency Building Fund drive, Penn State's first private fund-raising campaign. This was, however, only part of Thomas's grand plan to position Penn State as *the* state university. As such, it would be the capstone of Pennsylvania's public education system and the sole recipient of state appropriations for higher education, including $10,000,000 proposed for more new buildings.

Thomas's fund-raising initiative didn't bring in all the money needed, but the Tri-dorms (Watts, Irvin, and Jordan) were eventually built, along with the Ritenour Health Center, the Grange Building (a women's dorm), and Recreation Hall just west of New Beaver Field. Thomas, however, left after it became clear that his conflicts with economy-minded Governor Gifford Pinchot would not yield the kind of state support he envisioned.

THE DEPRESSION TO THE POSTWAR BOOM

Penn State entered the late 1920s with a new president, Ralph Dorn Hetzel, who brought to completion Thomas's building projects. In the early years of his presidency, a positive turn in Harrisburg's attitude toward Penn State and higher education in general brought additional new buildings to the campus core. These included Sackett Building, Buckhout and Borland Laboratories, Steidle Building, the Nittany Lion Inn, the Power Plant, and Henderson Building; additions to Pond Laboratory and Sparks Building; and a new Old Main to replace the crumbling original structure. All designed by Klauder, they continued the line of classical revival–style structures, with some variations. (While Klauder had become famous as the "Dean of Collegiate Gothic," designing gothic revival structures for other schools, the Georgian and classical revival styles were favored here because they were less expensive.)

Hetzel took advantage of the good times before the stock market crash, but the remainder of his term as president was focused on coping with the Great Depression, World War II, and the influx of veterans stimulated by the

GI Bill. Indeed, the University Park campus was directly affected not only by the depression of the 1930s but also by President Roosevelt's new approach to relief. His activist programs included several that would put men back to work by constructing needed public buildings.

Klauder had continued to revise his campus master plan as new buildings were added to the grounds. A substantial revision came in 1937 in anticipation of major federal funding for public works. To address the long-unmet need to accommodate more women students, Penn State had already funded construction of the Atherton Hall dormitory and the White Physical Education Building through loans. Now the school prepared for a building boom. The legislature created the General State Authority in 1937, and in the next year $5,000,000 from the federal Public Works Administration was funneled through the General State Authority to Penn State.

Construction of the Nittany Lion Inn

These funds built Pattee Library, Burrowes Building, Electrical Engineering West, Osmond and Frear Laboratories, the Agricultural Engineering Building, Ferguson Building, the Poultry Plant, and additions to Steidle and Sparks buildings. While these structures continued in Klauder's classical revival style, they tended to be more austere than his first works, with less dramatic ornamentation. Klauder died in 1938, and while the College continued to expand with the acquisition of the Mont Alto campus, Stone Valley, and more farmland, the central campus remained relatively compact. Virtually all of its buildings were still located within the original two hundred acres donated by General Irvin in 1855, bounded by Atherton Street, Park Avenue, Shortlidge Road, and College Avenue. To the west was the nine-hole golf course, laid out in 1921, and to the east stretched the experimental farms and plots with barns, greenhouses, and the federal Pasture Research Laboratory just across Shortlidge.

The postwar era brought thousands of veterans entering college, America's great suburban growth spurt, and later the baby boomers. Even before the war ended, veterans were flocking to campuses with their tuition and

Temporary housing from the late 1940s

support paid by the GI Bill of Rights. The sudden demand for enrollment at Penn State could not be met without dramatic steps being taken. Starting in 1946, several years' worth of freshmen were "farmed out" to the state teachers' colleges as well as Penn State undergraduate centers around the state. On campus, new permanent dormitories for men and women were being designed, and former army barracks and trailers became the temporary Pollock Circle and Windcrest Trailer Park. Inexpensive, prefabricated housing was built for students as Nittany Halls and for new faculty families as Eastview Terrace. In addition, a temporary classroom building (south of Grange Hall) and a temporary student union (north of Ritenour Health Center) were constructed. The classroom building was used for about seventeen years and was razed in 1964. The Temporary Union Building (or TUB), though, later became the Paul Robeson Cultural Center and survived until 2000.

GROWTH IN THE EISENHOWER AND WALKER YEARS, 1950–1970

Even as campus buildings began to extend out from the core campus, seven major academic buildings, plus North Halls, were built on central campus during the term of President Milton S. Eisenhower (1950–56), including Whitmore and Fenske Laboratories, Eisenhower Chapel, and the Hetzel Union Building (HUB). At the same time, the Graduate Circle Apartments, South Halls, most of Pollock Halls, and the first four dorms in East Halls—with their respective dining halls—along with the Home Management Houses and Wagner Building were built east of Shortlidge Road. These buildings, designed by architects chosen by the General State Authority, marked the transition from Klauder's classical revival style to modern architecture on campus. Comparatively plain and functional, they lacked ornament, their outer skins consisting largely of brick, rough-hewn limestone, or tinted metal panels.

These structures appeared in response to the university's regularly revised master plan, which kept increasing enrollment estimates. In 1954, an enrollment of eighteen thousand students was envisioned for 1970. Four years later, under new president Eric A. Walker (1956–70), the figure grew to twenty-five thousand students. By 1959, some fundamental changes to the campus had been planned, including the gradual move of the athletic plant from central to east campus as well as the development of a complex of research buildings on the east campus. In addition, new buildings for the colleges of Business Administration, Education, and Arts and Architecture were being planned in the central campus or on the golf course. With ever more distant dormitories, walking distance for students became an issue. In 1960, the university moved to a four-term system that included twenty-minute intervals between classes.

The 1960s saw the completion of much of the expansion needed to accommodate the enrollment growth. Two more units were added to Pollock Halls, while East Halls added ten dormitories and more dining hall/union facilities. Additionally, the Computer Building and Shields and Mitchell buildings all appeared across Shortlidge Road near the new dormitory areas. Plans to build on the golf course were gradually abandoned as additions and new buildings were inserted into central campus. Seventeen new structures were built for the colleges of Business, Arts, Science, Education, Liberal Arts, Engineering, and Earth and Mineral Sciences in the 1960s. In addition, the new Kern Graduate Union Building and Keller Conference Center were constructed, all of which created a near-urban density in the campus core—a density emphasized by the massive, unrelieved brick-box appearance of many of these buildings.

THE OSWALD AND JORDAN ADMINISTRATIONS, 1970–1990

In 1970, Penn State saw a new administration under President John W. Oswald, one that recognized the need for new academic and physical planning in the early 1970s. Enrollments continued to inch upward despite the growth of the Commonwealth Campus system, but financial aid for higher education from government sources was becoming severely limited. Enrollment for 1980 was projected at 32,500, and it was already clear that town-gown issues—transportation, student housing, and coordination with local government planning bodies—were becoming increasingly serious concerns. The 1974 campus development plan focused on renovating older buildings and proposed only a few additional structures on campus. No new student housing was planned, given students' increased interest in off-campus living and the inflationary costs of new dormitory construction. Environmental quality was highlighted, as was the need to restrain automobile access and promote bus and bicycle use, enhancing the pedestrian experience in the central core.

At the same time, the preservation of historic structures was guaranteed in 1970 when the Board of Trustees set aside the oldest core area surrounding Old Main, Schwab, Carnegie, University House, and Old Botany from future development. Later, more than forty buildings were designated as contributing structures to the Old Campus Complex and Ag Hill districts, which are on the National Register of Historic Places. These actions likely resulted from the replacement of the landmark Armory with the much-maligned Willard Building addition in 1964 and the threatened demolition of University House in 1970. (A firestorm of protest saved the oldest building on campus.)

Only nine major buildings were constructed in the 1970s—Eisenhower Auditorium, Althouse and Noll Laboratories, the Business Administration Building, Walker Building, Nursing, Agricultural Administration, Oswald Tower, and the IM (Intramural) Building—and all generally followed the trend of massive, brick-box design. By the end of the decade, it was believed that the building boom was over, and that major maintenance, utility upgrades, energy conservation, and provisions for handicapped access, combined with renovation and very limited replacement of outmoded structures, would be the agenda for the future. Under the administration of Bryce Jordan (1983–90), there was very little new construction. Many buildings were renovated and space reallocated.

While an interim planning document was prepared in 1977, the first major revision of the 1974 campus plan came in 1987. The context for this revision remained the steady growth of enrollment, which approached thirty-five thousand by 1985 and almost thirty-nine thousand by 1990. The 1987 study pointed to the need for expanding the Engineering buildings on the west campus and building a complex of buildings on the east campus, including a hotel as well as convocation, conference, alumni, and visitors' centers. In the central campus, the plan focused on replacing the Poultry Plant with athletic space and on constructing the Thomas and Agricultural Science and Industries Buildings, and possible adjacent structures, on recreational fields and parking lots. Also proposed were additions to the Nittany Lion Inn, the Music Building, Pattee Library, and the HUB (all of which were

The Museum of Art under construction in the 1970s

completed by 2000). While the concern for promoting a more pedestrian-friendly campus was echoed from earlier reports, this document also noted the pressing need for as many as three thousand additional parking spaces, due to overall growth. Ultimately, the HUB, the Nittany Lion Inn, and the Eisenhower parking garages were built to address this need.

A fundamental change that enabled these new structures also emerged during this period. The state mandated that University and private funds would be required to cover as much as 40 percent of the cost of such buildings, with the balance coming from the Commonwealth's capital budget. This gave the University more flexibility in initiating new building projects and, for the first time since the 1950s, a choice in architects.

THE 1990s—AND INTO THE FUTURE

Given the steady enrollment growth in the 1990s (along with concurrent growth in the faculty and staff complement), additional buildings were constructed to meet specific opportunities, such as the Wartik Laboratory for biotechnology research and the Mateer Building for an expanding School of Hospitality Management. After some hesitation, construction began as well on the west campus with the Hallowell Building, renovation of the foods building for Engineering and Earth and Mineral Sciences, and additional buildings for the Applied Research Laboratory and engineering research.

On the east campus, joint state and University funding and philanthropy created the Bryce Jordan Center, while some of the other buildings initially proposed for that immediate area instead became the anchor for the Penn State Research Park to the east of the State College bypass—including the Penn Stater Conference Center Hotel, along with business incubator and research buildings. The Alumni Center was finally designed as a striking complementary addition to the rear of University House, placing that facility in a convenient, central location. Additional athletic facilities have been built or upgraded to meet Penn State's needs for facilities that match or surpass the competitive quality of those of other Big Ten institutions.

As the 1990s drew to a close, the University continued to eye very specific additions to the building stock of the campus. The master plan submitted to the Board of Trustees in March 1999 is probably the most extensive planning document yet created for the University. Its primary goals—creating a pedestrian-oriented core, moving parking to the periphery, continuing infill rather than extending sprawl, preserving and increasing green spaces, and promoting alternatives to traditional vehicles—focus on land use by creating a fabric of buildings and civic spaces that enhance the pedestrian experience.

Some new academic buildings have been fitted into the central core, but more new academic and residential space has been built in a carefully defined portion of the old White Golf Course west of Atherton Street as well as to the east of Shortlidge Road, and agricultural and athletic spaces there have shifted even farther eastward. Special attention is being given to "green design" in new buildings and, in particular, to those structures situated where the university and town meet, in an effort to create a welcoming and porous interface.

Most dramatic in realizing these plans has been the progress on the Five-Year Capital Construction Plan covering the fiscal years 2001/2–2005/6. Including new construction, renovations, and utility improvements, this plan projected spending $769 million on these projects over the five years. And as of Penn State's sesquicentennial year, most of the major projects envisioned are complete, in construction, or will begin fairly close to the schedule that had been set. Already finished and/or occupied by the beginning of 2004 were the Beaver Stadium addition and renovations, the west campus graduate and family housing, the MBNA Career Services Building, the Pasquerilla Spiritual Center, the Information Science and Technology Building, and the Chemistry

Building. These and the structures to follow represent the most significant physical expansion of the campus since the 1960s.

Yet in spite of the turmoil of construction, the quality of the campus experience remains paramount for the planners and the University. The stress is on an environment that can integrate teaching, research, and outreach; that enriches the vibrancy of students' learning experiences; and that preserves and enhances the memorable campus that is historical, rural, human-scaled, walkable, and welcoming. The challenges to achieving this are numerous (the almost urban-sized population and the widespread scale of the campus among them). Indeed, while the storied rural isolation of University Park is still widely accepted, it becomes more myth than reality every day. Nevertheless, the campus's eclectic architecture, diverse plantings, trees, and landscapes, views of surrounding mountains and valley, and easy access to—but distinct boundary with—a community that many consider the "quintessential college town" remain powerful for Pennsylvanians and Penn State alumni across the globe.

College Avenue, 1905

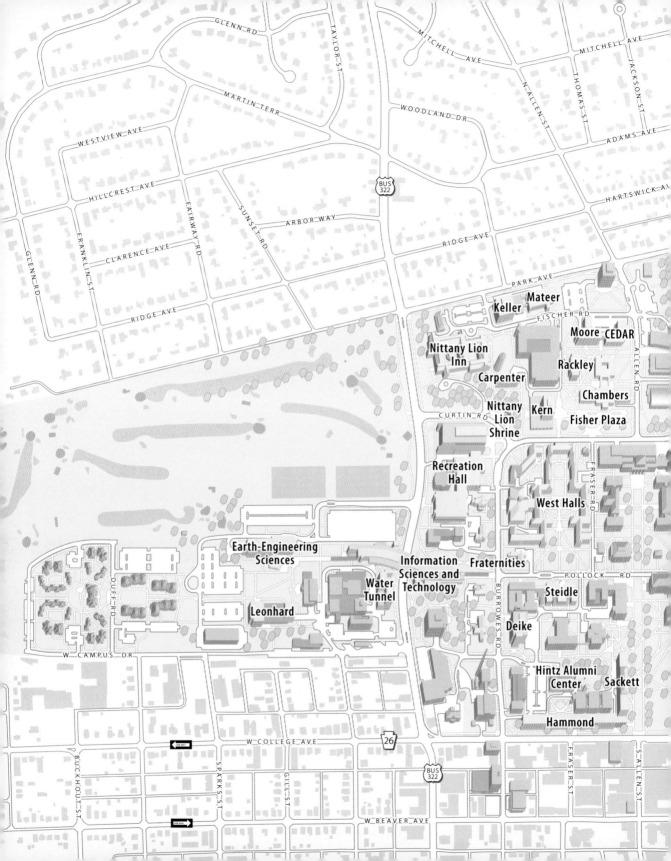

WEST CAMPUS

Hintz Family Alumni Center · Steidle Building · West Halls
Social Sciences · Keller/Mateer Buildings · Nittany Lion Inn · Nittany Lion Shrine
Recreation Hall · Burrowes Fraternities · Information Sciences and Technology Building
Leonhard/Earth and Engineering Sciences Buildings · Sackett/Hammond Buildings

I HINTZ FAMILY ALUMNI CENTER (2001)

In the words of its architects, the Hintz Family Alumni Center represents "respect for tradition and engagement in the future." The center is newly designed, but it incorporates what was, for nearly a century, the college president's official residence on campus. Built in 1864 for the first Penn State president, Evan Pugh, President's House was only the second building—after the College Building—to grace the campus. In the 1880s and 1890s, the house saw extensive renovations, as porches and a third floor were added. One porch carefully wound around an apple tree beloved by Frances Atherton, the wife of George W. Atherton, Penn State's seventh president.

By the 1940s, President's House had begun to resemble a southern plantation, with a sizeable portico with two-story columns. Milton S. Eisenhower, Penn State's president from 1950 to 1956 and brother of U.S. president Dwight Eisenhower, would leave the porch light on as a gesture of welcome to passersby. But by 1970, when students protested the Vietnam War on the grounds of President's House (also known as University House), the building needed major renovations and no longer seemed suitable as the university president's home.

Today, the Alumni Center welcomes visiting alumni and houses the Alumni Association's offices. The 43,000-square-foot facility, which was dedicated in April 2001, is named after Ed Hintz and his family. An Alumni Fellow and a Distinguished Alumnus of the University, Hintz became president of Penn State's Board of Trustees in January 2001. More than 430 donors helped fund the $9.5-million construction of the center. The architects, Thomas Purdy and Linda O'Gwynn of Purdy O'Gwynn Barnhart Architects, are themselves Penn State alumni.

Along with such amenities as three working fireplaces and the southern courtyard shown here (with a sitting wall built of limestone from the old University House garage), the Alumni Center also prominently features inscriptions of the four stanzas of the Penn State alma mater. The first can be found in skylit Robb Hall, on the first floor. The second stanza appears at the entrance to the building; the third, at the end of the conference room. The fourth stanza appears in the flagstone visitors cross as they leave the Alumni Center: "May our lives but swell thy fame, / Dear old State, dear old State."

· · · · ·

150,000 Lions Can't Be Wrong

In 1870, the Penn State Alumni Association sprang into existence, with Professor A. A. Breneman (Class of '66—that's 1866) as its first president. Twelve Penn Staters attended that inaugural meeting in a chemistry room on the first floor of Old Main. Today, the Penn State Alumni Association is the largest dues-paying alumni association in the United States, with more than 150,000 members who support the University's mission of teaching, research, and service. It comprises 280 chartered groups throughout the country, providing opportunities for professional development, networking, volunteering, and friendship building. The Alumni Association sponsors University athletic programs and homecoming events, endows local and national scholarships, and organizes domestic and international travel programs for its members. Truly, there are Penn Staters EVERYWHERE!

BEING A NATIVE OF Centre County, I was destined to be a Penn Stater. Whether spending football Saturdays at Beaver Stadium, watching my big brother play for Joe Paterno, attending PSU as an undergraduate and graduate student, attending Penn State conferences, serving on the University's College of Education Board of Directors and the Graduate School Alumni Society Board of Directors, volunteering for activities, walking through campus, or getting ice cream from the Creamery, I've always been Penn State proud.

After being away for ten years, I moved back to Bellefonte, and my new home gives me another PSU connection. The house was built for Rebecca Valentine Pugh, Penn State's first First Lady—wife of the first president of Penn State, Dr. Evan Pugh. For Evan and Rebecca, it was love at first sight. Rebecca was beautiful, intelligent, and fluent in German. They were married on February 4, 1864. His wedding gift to her was a watch, which she wore on a metal chain with links filled with gold filigree.

My Penn State memorabilia seem so appropriate in this house, and I look forward to making more Penn State memories and connections.

—MARIANNE E. HAZEL,
CLASSES OF '90 AND '95

Steidle Building, now the home of the Department of Materials Science and Engineering, is a classical revival–style structure with a semicircular portico topped by a copper dome. It was designed by Charles Z. Klauder and named for Edward Steidle, founding dean of the College of Earth and Mineral Sciences (1928–53). Steidle was an alumnus of Penn State's Class of 1911 and came to the College from the Carnegie Institute of Technology. Soon after taking the deanship, Steidle had the school's name changed from Mines and Metallurgy to Mineral Industries, highlighting his sense that its purview would expand well beyond coal mining. In 1930, the school completed construction of a new brick-and-limestone Mineral Industries Building (later to become Steidle Building). Under Steidle's leadership, the School of Mineral Industries entered into partnerships with other academic and industry groups—and Steidle was so successful at promoting mineral industries education that the Pennsylvania General Assembly changed the University's charter in 1939 to make the state's secretary of mines a fourth ex officio member of the Board of Trustees.

Visitors will want to explore the Earth and Mineral Sciences Museum and Art Gallery, long housed in Steidle Building and recently moved to upgraded quarters in nearby Deike Building. The museum galleries feature eye-catching minerals and fossils—including amazonite crystals from Colorado, a case of stunning agates, and a hadrosaur "footprint"—as well as displays on Pennsylvania mining and historical mining equipment. The museum also maintains the Steidle Collection of paintings and sculpture depicting mining and related industries. This extensive collection numbers more than three hundred

artworks, including Roy Hilton's *Miner*, shown here. Steidle established the collection in the 1930s to enhance the school and to draw attention to the mineral industries. He was known to be a man of eclectic interests—and among the museum's more unusual holdings are mastodon tusks, an enormous diplodocus bone, and two shrunken heads from the Jivaro Indians of Ecuador.

· · · · ·

Penn State's First President

A thirty-one-year-old agricultural chemist and Chester County native, Evan Pugh was named president of the Farmers' High School (later named the Agricultural College of Pennsylvania) in February 1859. During his tenure as Penn State's formidable first president, Pugh, pictured here, defended his educational ideals against political criticism and fiercely lobbied the state for increased funding. He dispensed harsh discipline to students who, lured from their studies by the card games and liquor parlors of nearby Bellefonte, broke his strict curfew. He died on April 29, 1864, reportedly from typhoid fever and complications of a broken arm. A long line of dedicated presidents has followed—though happily for students, the curfew has since been dropped!

Evan Pugh	1859–64	John Martin Thomas	1921–25
William Henry Allen	1864–66	Ralph Dorn Hetzel	1927–47
John Fraser	1866–68	James Milholland (acting)	1947–50
Thomas Henry Burrowes	1868–71	Milton Stover Eisenhower	1950–56
James Calder	1871–80	Eric A. Walker	1956–70
Joseph Shortlidge	1880–81	John W. Oswald	1970–83
James Y. McKee (acting)	1881–82	Bryce Jordan	1983–90
George W. Atherton	1882–1906	Joab Thomas	1990–95
James A. Beaver (acting)	1906–8	Graham Spanier	1995–present
Edwin Erle Sparks	1908–20		

3 WEST HALLS

Irvin, Watts, Jordan (1922–37) | Hamilton, Thompson, McKee (1949) | Waring (1950)

College students and alumni often recall their dorm experiences as formative ones. Penn Staters may be surprised to learn, then, that in the latter half of the nineteenth century students and faculty lived in the original Old Main. This Old Main held dining facilities, classrooms, the library, and the president's office as well as living quarters. Students at the time studied by candlelight or oil lamps, which they paid for out of their own pockets.

Of course, much has changed for students living on campus! Today, Penn State dormitories feature the now-traditional desk, bed, closet, and telephone, as well as state-of-the-art computer connectivity and, of course, the microfridge. The microfridge represents a practical response to a perennial problem. In the relatively recent past, Penn Staters could expect to find their dorm rooms each supplied with a refrigerator/freezer, but a number of students also brought microwaves to satisfy their popcorn and mac-and-cheese cravings. (More rarely, they actually heated leftover pizza for breakfast.) When these various appliances drew from the same outlets, they posed electrical hazards, leading the Housing Office to phase out the old refrigerator/freezers and bring in the single-plug microfridge in the early 1990s.

Despite the common features of campus dorm rooms, Penn State's residence halls have distinct personalities. The West Halls area, seen in this aerial photo, was built in three stages and largely designed by Charles Z. Klauder. It is Georgian revival in style, with buildings arranged around an open quadrangle of three stepped courtyards with symmetrical walkways and arches. Like many residence halls, West Halls provides computer facilities along with dining commons and study lounges. Art exhibitions appear in the West Halls Lounge. And to enhance students' on-campus living experiences further, the West Halls Residence Association sponsors events throughout the year, including study breaks, open mike nights, and broomball tournaments—the latter involving the heady trio of brooms, ice, and injury.

4 SOCIAL SCIENCES

Chambers Building (1960) | Rackley Building (1963) | Moore Building (1968) | Kern Building (1969) | CEDAR Building (1970) | Carpenter Building (1971)

These buildings, clustered together near Allen Road, serve the College of Education, the Departments of Psychology and Economics (College of the Liberal Arts), and the Graduate School. Like the buildings in the Eberly College of Science area near the HUB, they testify to the historic boom in undergraduate enrollment that set off a wave of new construction in the 1960s and 1970s. The buildings are loosely positioned around Fisher Plaza. During the 1930s and 1940s, the plaza area held tennis courts that were flooded in the winter for ice skating. Now, visitors can relax on the plaza's benches, appreciate the flowers, and sometimes even enjoy a summertime concert. This restful space, planted with trees and shrubs, was named for Penn State alumnus Herman G. Fisher, the founder and former president of Fisher-Price Toys.

IN THE FALL of 1956, I was assigned to Thompson Hall, as were many female freshmen. The male freshmen were assigned to Hamilton Hall, located across the courtyard from Thompson.

Every evening, several hundred other freshman girls and I walked to the Waring Dining Hall, which was located in the men's dormitory. We had to walk through the "line-up" of young men along the sidewalk and endure such flattering comments as "I'll date you if you lose fifteen pounds." Some girls took the long route around the buildings to avoid the fun and frivolity.

One spring morning in 1957, I noticed that the trees in the courtyard were sprouting white "leaves." The trees had been decorated with feminine personal pads.

The next year, Penn State Housing moved all of the female residents to the newly constructed South Halls and made West Halls all male. It was the end of the West Halls line-up.

—ELIZABETH CARTER FIDA, CLASS OF '60

Chambers, the main administrative building for the College of Education, dates from 1960 and was named in 1962 after Will Grant Chambers, the first dean of the College of Education. Leaving through its rear doors, visitors will find a charming courtyard decorated with sculptures. The courtyard's plantings attract vivid butterflies in warm weather. Chambers features a two-story lobby, where students often congregate, and its front doors open onto Fisher Plaza, as these pictures show.

Behind Chambers is the CEDAR Building. (The acronym stands for Center for Education, Diagnosis, and Remediation, which was housed there when the building was erected in 1970.) Today, CEDAR is home to two departments in the College of Education that aim to understand and improve school systems by combining the study of education with the study of psychology and the many problems children may face. The CEDAR School Psychology Clinic, located on the first floor, offers services to children, adolescents, and young adults while giving firsthand experience to budding school psychologists. Connected to CEDAR is Moore, which was built in 1968 and dedicated in 1972. It took the name of Bruce V. Moore, head of the Department of Psychology (1928–52), and today it houses that renowned department.

Just beyond Fisher Plaza is Rackley, built in 1963 and named for J. Ralph Rackley, a professor of education and former provost. Rackley houses the Department of Education Policy Studies along with many essential programs concerned with literacy and higher education. The department's American Indian Leadership Program, established in 1970, is commemorated with a historical marker recognizing it as the oldest and most successful program of its kind. Located on Rackley's fourth floor is the Center for the Study of Higher Education, one of the nation's first research centers created for the sole purpose of studying postsecondary educational policy issues.

Kern Graduate Center, built in 1969, serves as a headquarters for the Graduate School at Penn State—one of the largest graduate schools in the nation, with more than 10,000 students. The building was named after Frank D. Kern, the first dean of the Graduate School. In the Kern lobby, the Graduate Commons features a variety of displays and artworks, including George Sam Gardner's *Bomb #7*, as well as an information center and the popular Otto's Café. Kern also houses a number of classrooms and offices, including space for the Department of Economics (College of the Liberal Arts) and the Faculty Senate. Behind Kern to the west stands Carpenter Building, built in 1971. Carpenter houses the Anthropology Department and the Matson Museum of Anthropology, which features archeological and anthropological collections from across the globe. The building's name honors C. R. Carpenter, a celebrated scholar in psychology and anthropology.

5 KELLER BUILDING (1964) / MATEER BUILDING (1993)

Inside Keller Building's front doors lies a spacious lobby with a back wall made entirely of glass. Visible behind this wall is Keller's most prominent office, the name of which is etched across the frosted lower third of the giant window: Pennsylvania State University Continuing and Distance Education. Founded by J. Orvis Keller, Penn State's director of General Extension (1916–53), the Continuing Education office now serves more than 187,000 people each year and is one of the nation's largest programs of its kind. Keller Building also houses such offices as the Arts and Health Outreach Initiative, the Collaborative and Active Learning Institute, and the Institute for the Study of Adult Literacy.

Adjoining Keller is Mateer Building, shown here, named for State College philanthropists and restaurateurs Laura and Marlin "Matty" Mateer and home to the School of Hospitality Management (College of Health and Human Development). Designed by John M. Kostecky Jr. and Associates, Mateer Building offers HM students a chance to do much more than learn the theoretical aspects of their field. Thanks to corporate sponsors such as Hoss's Steak and Sea House and Yuengling Brewery, the building features state-of-the-art laboratory facilities, the cornerstone of which is the Mateer Research Kitchen.

Mateer's most striking architectural feature is the semicircle that juts out of its east side. Inside is the glass-walled dining room of Café Laura, a fully realized restaurant where HM students practice planning, marketing, preparing, and serving meals to the public. The restaurant sees a brisk business weekdays for breakfast and lunch, but its biggest attractions are its periodic theme dinners. Planned and executed by the HM program's upperclassmen, these multicourse meals have imaginatively sent diners to the islands of Greece or the Caribbean, to Tuscany, to California wine country or New Orleans—and even along historic Route 66.

6 NITTANY LION INN (1931; MAJOR RENOVATIONS 1952, 1970, 1991)

In 1929, despite national economic panic, The Pennsylvania State College and the surrounding area were growing rapidly. Meetings and conferences alone drew roughly 1,500 visitors each month; alumni, too, came for sporting events and other campus affairs. Along with the visiting families of the College's 4,000 students, they overwhelmed State College's ninety existing hotel rooms. On May 1, 1930, workers broke ground for the Nittany Lion Inn, and almost one year to the day later, the $3.50-per-night rooms opened to the public. The hotel's grand main entrance, pictured here, remains much the same as it looked that spring some seventy-five years ago.

This Dutch Colonial Revival hotel was designed not to serve as mere lodging but to evoke a fine yet informal, home-away-from-home feeling. All areas of the Inn were thoughtfully decorated, and in addition to the expected bed and dresser, every guest room featured a writing desk, a pewter table lamp, an upholstered armchair, and a blanket chest.

The first guests enjoyed six-course meals and danced to the Varsity Ten in what President Eric Walker would later call "Penn State's living room." These guests received a personal invitation from the Inn's general manager and paid $5 to participate in the one-night gala that marked the grand opening. A few weeks later, members of student organizations and fraternity officers were invited to attend an evening's introduction to the Inn. They paid $2.50 for the festivities, including dinner, dancing, and late refreshments.

The Inn served as the social center of campus until the outbreak of World War II, when it became the headquarters for members of both the Navy's V-12 officer training program and the Armed Services Training Program. After the war, the military programs vacated the site, but the idea of using the Inn for auxiliary purposes had caught on. Soon, students studying hotel and restaurant management were gaining real-world work experience at the Inn—from answering the phones to working in the kitchen.

Several renovations have occurred to the Inn over the years. Between 1931 and the early 1950s, for example, the number of rooms in the Inn doubled. The last major renovation added eighty new rooms, more expansive meeting space, and the popular Whiskers lounge.

· · · · ·

Penn State Firsts, 1855–1900

1857   Construction began on Penn State's first building—"old" Old Main.

1859   February 16 saw the first day of classes for the Farmers' High School of Pennsylvania, with a faculty of four. Sixty-nine of the 119 students enrolled for the first year were present.

1861   The first class graduated. In December, 11 students—the first to complete a baccalaureate program at an American agricultural college—received a Bachelor of Scientific Agriculture degree.

1870   The Alumni Association was organized, with Professor A. A. Breneman, Class of '66, as its first president.

1871   The first women students were admitted. These six women were overseen by the first preceptress, Mary E. Butterfield.

1873   Rebecca Hannah Ewing was the first woman to graduate.

1887   The first biennial state appropriation of $100,000 provided original maintenance funds and launched the earliest major building program. New buildings included the Armory, Old Botany, the Chemistry and Physics

I NEVER HAD any doubt about finding love at Penn State—the question was finding the one, true, "forever" love.

My high school boyfriend moved into Sproul at the start of my junior year of high school. I had sworn off big universities, certain I would end up at some tiny school. But as I helped him move in, I fell in love with Penn State and decided that it was the place for me! Two and a half years later, I was a freshman living in Stone—and ending the relationship with the boy from high school. Not to worry: I had my eye on a certain guy in my English 15 class who lived in Mifflin. By the end of our junior year, though, with me in Simmons and him in Gateway Apartments, we decided that we were better off as friends.

So there I was, ready to start my senior year, thinking about the future, and all without a boy of my own. The day I moved into Thompson, my mom walked me to the steps in front of Chambers. As we sat there, she told me that my perfect guy was at Penn State. I just hadn't met him yet. She added that she had complete confidence that he and I would find each other. Less than a week later, I met him in the dining commons of West Halls. His name was Jeff, and he was rooming with my friend Brad in Hamilton. It didn't take long to figure out that I had met my perfect match! Jeff and I have definitely had our share of ups and downs, yet I know with all my heart that I found my one true love in the dining commons at Penn State.

—AMANDA LUKENS, CLASS OF '00

Laboratory, Engineering Building, Ladies' Cottage, Experiment Station, and faculty residences.

1888 Phi Gamma Delta, the first permanently established men's national fraternity on campus, was chartered.

1889 The first edition of La Vie, the college yearbook, was published.

1892 The first "stadium," Old Beaver Field—named for James A. Beaver, president of the Board of Trustees, Pennsylvania governor, and Civil War general—was completed.

1892 The first correspondence courses, called the "Chautauqua Course in Agriculture," were offered.

1896 Lawrence M. Colfelt, D.D., was appointed as the first chaplain.

THIS IS THE OTHER side of the coin: living at home in State College versus in the dorms on campus. I was a State College High School graduate among my peers entering Penn State in September 1940. Many of us had college-professor parents. I still lived under parents' rules but matured socially. I had easier times getting campus jobs, worked at the library from 5:00 to 7:00 p.m. while other students were eating in the dining halls, and waited tables in the dorms and at the Nittany Lion Inn. Joining Alpha Chi Omega sorority provided me with campus life.

The year 1941 was a turning point. With World War II starting, Penn State received an influx of military personnel, their temporary stay lasting two to three months. The Navy sent two hundred ensigns every sixteen weeks, and that is how I met and later married my first husband, now deceased. Air Force personnel sang as they marched to classes. The USO formed and dances were held Saturday nights in the Armory. There were ration books and shortages. There were no department stores in State College,

7 NITTANY LION SHRINE (1942)

Said to be the most photographed place on the University Park campus—and pictured here, too—the Nittany Lion Shrine sits atop a small mound set back from the sidewalk of Curtin Road near Rec Hall. The gift of the Class of 1940 funded the thirteen-ton block of Indiana limestone, along with the services of famed sculptor Heinz Warneke, who, to borrow an old joke, took the massive slab of stone and chipped away everything that didn't look like a Nittany Lion.

The Lion Shrine is always a popular site, but at certain times of year it sees uncharacteristically large crowds. On graduation weekends, hundreds of students line up to have their photos taken in commencement regalia with the famous stone lion. Homecoming brings the annual Guard the Lion Shrine campaign, led by the Lion Ambassadors. The annual camp-out has its origins in the homecoming of 1966, Joe Paterno's first year of coaching football at Penn State. Morale for the homecoming game against Syracuse was low, and in an effort to rally school spirit, Paterno's wife, Sue, and a friend went to the Shrine in the dead of night and painted it orange—a supposed

affront by rival fans. Penn State went on to win the game, and the water-based paint washed off easily. But the following year, inspired by Paterno's hoax, several Syracuse fans caused real damage to the lion, covering it in oil-based paint and chipping one of its ears. Spurred by the vandalism, the Lion Ambassadors resolved to protect the lion on homecoming weekends from then on. Over the years, the lion's ears have been prone to repeated damage. In 1979, Warneke worked with the head stonecutter of the Washington National Cathedral, Vincenzo Palumbo, to replace an ear broken by vandals a year earlier; again in 1994, the lion's ear required Palumbo's attention. In the summer of 2003, the ear came off once more, but according to a police spokesman, "It was the same break from before. It wasn't done intentionally."

• • • • •

The Man and the Suit

Necessity is the mother of invention and so, in 1904, when senior H. D. "Joe" Mason realized that his school had no counterpart to the famous Princeton Tiger, he invented one. "Every college the world over of any consequence has a college emblem of some kind—all but The Pennsylvania State College. . . . Why not select for ours the king of beasts—the Lion! Dignified, courageous,

so I'd go to Altoona for a prom dress. This was the Big Band era, when dancing to music of Glenn Miller, Tommy Dorsey, and Gene Krupa would put us "in the mood" to forget the war. The Corner Room and the College Diner were both favorite gathering places. We went swimming at Whipple Dam and Greenwood Furnace and, for an extra thrill, we danced up at Sky Top. Christmas holidays provided resident students with fraternities available for dances for those whose fathers had been members during their college years. Taking advantage of the summer-accelerated semester, I graduated early, said goodbye to State College, and accepted a position with Goodyear Tire and Rubber Company in Akron, Ohio, a company heavily involved in the war effort. State College and Penn State have expanded so much since then, with new housing areas developed, yet still are the most beautiful college town and campus ever! Yes, it is still my town, my alma mater!

—JANET HENNINGER LOGAN,
CLASS OF '43

magnificent, the Lion allegorically represents all that our College Spirit should be, so why not 'the Nittany Mountain Lion,' as the eternal sentinel?" By 1907, the Nittany Lion had become Penn State's de facto mascot, though only with the unveiling of the Lion Shrine in 1942 did its adoption become official.

In 1922, however—around the time that two stuffed mountain lions were placed in Rec Hall to watch over athletic events—a student dressed in a furry lion suit first appeared at a football game. Senior Dick Hoffman wore his lion costume from a production of George Bernard Shaw's *Androcles and the Lion* to entertain fans at the Polo Grounds in a game against Syracuse. Early incarnations of "the suit" were actually made from the skin of its real-life counterpart, *Felis concolor*. Later suits were made of patched-together rabbit pelts, sometimes mended, according to legend, with remnants from someone's lamb coat. The switch from real to fake fur was made in 1952. Today, the costume is crafted from butterscotch-brown faux fur, with reinforced knees and strategically placed zippers and Velcro—but no pockets. Ears and tails are replaced often, more due to overzealous Penn State fans than wear and tear. Once politely described as "odoriferous," the twenty-pound sweat-soaked costume is hand-cleaned after every game.

· · · · ·

Nittany Lion Mascots

Richard Hoffman	1921?–23	Alfred Klimcke	1954–57
Leon Skinner	1927	William Hillgartner	1957–58
Eugene Wettstone	1939	John Behler	1957–60
Donald Newberry	1939?	Jack Lesyk	1960–61
George Terwilliger	1939–40	Unknown	1961–62
Tom Kelly	1941?–42	Paul Seltzer	1962–64
Robert Ritzmann	1942–44	Edwin Parkinson	1964–65
Peter Bates	1945–46	Martin Serota	1965–67
Clark Sharon	1946?–47	Danny Kohlhepp	1967–69
Wendell Lomady	1947–49	David Lacey	1969–71
Michael Kurowski	1949–50	David Brazet	1971–72
John Waters	1950–51	James Schaude	1972–73
Alex Gregal	1951–54	Robert Welsh	1973–75

Andrew Bailey	1975–77	Tim Durant	1991–93
Cliff Fiscus	1977–78	Richard Williams	1993–95
Norman Constantine	1978–80	Brad Cornali	1995–96
Roy Scott	1980–82	Nick Indeglio	1996–98
David Dailey	1982–84	Marty Duff	1998–2000
Robert Sterling	1984–86	Chuck Kimble	2000–2002
Doug Skinner	1986–88	Mike Zollars	2002–3
Peter Garland	1988–90	Stephen Soung	2003–5
Todd Shilkret	1990–91	Dave Johnson	2005–7

For more on the Nittany Lion mascot, see The Nittany Lion: An Illustrated Tale, by Jackie R. Esposito and Steven L. Herb (Penn State Press).

DURING MY FIRST fall trimester at Penn State's main campus, my parents came to visit and we made the always popular trek to see the Nittany Lion statue. My parents and a few of their friends were walking a bit ahead of me and my cohorts when I heard my dad say, "Hi, Joe!"

Now I'm thinking . . . we're over two hundred miles away from Philadelphia. Who in the world does my father know in State College?!

I look up to see Joe Paterno walking toward the group, shaking hands with my dad and the others. My dad was thrilled and has told that story a million times to anyone who would listen. He always made sure to say how wonderful it was that a legend like Joe Paterno was really just a "regular guy."

Here's to two regular guys who have both brought me many happy memories.

—PATRICIA PANZERA, CLASS OF '77

8 RECREATION HALL (1929; MAJOR RENOVATIONS 1953, 1965; CURRENT RENOVATION TO BE COMPLETED BY 2006)

THON, basketball, wrestling, gymnastics, volleyball: for many Penn State fans, athletic events define "Rec" Hall. The Georgian revival structure—the main entrance of which is pictured here—was designed by Charles Z. Klauder to "harmonize" with other new buildings on campus. Its construction, however, was anything but harmonious. In 1918, athletic director Hugo Bezdek

OF ALL THE PENN STATE experiences that I am proud of—and there are a lot of them—the one that sticks out as the most important thing I have ever been a part of is the Penn State Dance Marathon. I had no idea what I was getting into when I volunteered to dance as a freshman. Those forty-eight hours were the most grueling, most trying, most emotional, most exhilarating of my life. It was physically the most difficult thing I've ever experienced, including childbirth. But during those two days, I fell in love with the event and all that it stood for. THON went on to become a major part of my college career.

At my sophomore Dance Marathon, when I was on the Morale Committee, I met my future husband, Larry ('89)—although romance was the furthest thing from my mind at the time. The following two years I concentrated on helping my sorority, Alpha Sigma Alpha, along with Alpha Sigma Phi (my husband's fraternity), win the Greek money-raising division, which we did consistently for a decade. Our slogan was

implored Penn State to begin a subscription campaign to raise funds for the building, but the drive nearly failed until Rec Hall was included in the Emergency Building Fund Campaign of 1922. It would replace the old Armory facility, which dated from 1889. (The Armory, which stood where Willard Building now does, was razed in 1964.) The 1928 *Alumni News* noted that the new recreation building would not only provide increased floor area for physical education (as shown here) and athletic competitions but would also handle "large convocations, such as Commencement Exercises and Conventions."

When Rec Hall was built, it was one of the most lauded field houses in the country. It was dedicated on March 23, 1929. Between 1929 and 1996, when the Bryce Jordan Center opened, it was the home of Penn State's basketball program and was the main athletic events center on campus. On December 5, 1973, the largest crowd in Rec Hall history—8,600 people—witnessed the Nittany Lions defeat the Virginia Cavaliers. Indeed, the building has hosted scores of athletic events, including twenty collegiate national championships, international gymnastics competitions, twelve women's basketball championship tournaments, and, most recently, the Men's NCAA volleyball championships in May 2002. But the history of Rec Hall is more than sporting history. A circus—with participants from the School of Physical Education and Athletics—took place there in 1939, with clowns, feats of strength, and trapeze work. Bandleader Fred Waring performed there in 1956. In 1965, Dr. Martin Luther King Jr. addressed an audience of 9,000 people in its main

gym. And THON, the Penn State dance marathon that is also the largest philanthropic effort run by students, has been held in Rec Hall since 1999.

• • • • •

Dancing the Night (and Day, and Night, and Day) Away

Instituted to give the image of the Interfraternity Council a boost, Penn State's Dance Marathon was first held in the HUB Ballroom in 1973. Initially, THON was a competition that split proceeds between the marathon winners and a charity. In 1977, that charity was The Four Diamonds Fund, a Hershey, Pennsylvania—based philanthropy aimed at helping children diagnosed with cancer at the Penn State Children's Hospital. By 1978, interest in the competitive aspect of the marathon had waned, and the relationship between THON and The Four Diamonds Fund became permanent and exclusive, with all money raised being donated to the charity. Steady increases in the number of participants necessitated a move to the Mary Beaver White Building in 1979, but even then THON continued to grow—and moved to Rec Hall in 1999, as the above photo shows.

Every February, this "no-sitting, no-sleeping" forty-eight-hour event involves more than 10,000 students. The largest student-run philanthropy in the world, THON has raised over $30 million to help children and families battle pediatric cancer over the years.

"For the kids we can." And "can" we did! We had the whole process of "canning" down to a science. For three weekends in February, we would climb into cars and scatter across Pennsylvania and the Washington, D.C., area to collect money at the busiest intersections we could find. Armed with nothing but cardboard signs and tennis ball cans, we'd wait for the traffic lights to turn red, jump off the curb, and run through the lines of cars. Amazingly, people would readily roll down their windows and hand us cash. In hindsight, it was dangerous work, but it paid off. During one weekend, one carload of people could easily come home with thousands of dollars in change. When I was co-chair of the ASA/Alpha Sig team in 1989, we became the first organization to break the $100,000 mark for THON. It remains one of my proudest accomplishments.

—KAREN MILLER WALKER,
CLASS OF '89

IN THE EARLY 1940s, the U.S. Navy became keenly aware that its methods to produce naval officers—the Naval Academy and college ROTC programs—could not fill the many positions opening up as it rapidly expanded to meet the needs of a world at war. From this need the V-12 program was born.

A nationwide test was given on April 2, 1943, to 315,952 male high school seniors. Those who passed with the highest scores were invited to participate in the program and received a commission and a two-year college education at no cost. Those who didn't pass were left to the draft boards. At the recommendation of my brother George, I took that test and, after completing the necessary physical, I received notice that I was assigned to complete the college portion of my training at Penn State.

On the afternoon of June 30, 1943, a Greyhound bus delivered me to the Post House on Atherton Street. I noted Rec Hall from the bus window, then set off on foot to make it my first stop. Entering the gym, I was greeted by a game of badminton

9 BURROWES FRATERNITIES

The forty-five houses used by Penn State's fraternities constitute some of the most ornate architecture anywhere in State College. Particularly on Fraternity Row, south of Beaver Avenue, the buildings, which largely date from the 1920s and 1930s, often look more like mansions or castles than dwellings suitable for college students. Only five fraternity houses are physically located on campus—those of Alpha Zeta, Beta Theta Pi, Phi Delta Theta (pictured here), Phi Gamma Delta, and Sigma Nu, all on Burrowes Road—and each has a ninety-nine-year lease with the University.

Penn State's Greek system is one of the nation's foremost, with more than sixty fraternities and twenty-six sororities. Yet it had a humble beginning—one that came "strictly from hunger." The fraternities began as an outgrowth of student eating clubs organized in the 1800s to supplement overburdened campus dining facilities, and they gradually took on a fraternal quality, each club having its own name and special cheers. The Greek movement at Penn State had a false start in 1872, when a chapter of Delta Tau Delta was set up and promptly banned by the faculty. The faculty and trustees strongly opposed the idea of fraternities, seeing them as "corrupting," and in 1873 the faculty voted for "such action on Secret Fraternities as to prevent their future existence in the College." But owing to strong pressure on the part of students and alumni, growing numbers of faculty who were themselves fraternity alumni, and increasingly crowded campus housing, administrators rescinded the ban on fraternities in the spring of 1887. By the following year, chapters of two national fraternal organizations (Phi Gamma Delta and Beta Theta Pi) had established a presence at Penn State, and by 1904, the college had decided to set aside a handful of campus lots for fraternity buildings. By 1906, Phi Delta Theta had built a stately three-story brick and sandstone house, graced with a wide veranda and several fireplaces, on one of these lots.

Penn State's fraternities have undergone many changes through the years, particularly in times of national hardship. During World War II, the fraternity houses served as barracks for military trainees (seen here marching up Burrowes Street). After the war, the influx of returning veterans, many of them fraternity members or students wanting to join the Greek-letter groups, posed a housing problem. This led to the expansion of many chapters and the founding of eight new fraternities.

Today, about 12 percent of the total undergraduate population belongs to a Greek organization. Both fraternities and sororities provide social events for their members and conduct many charitable fund-raising events throughout the year to benefit local and national causes. The famous Interfraternity Council/Panhellenic Dance Marathon, known to Penn Staters as THON, is the largest student-run philanthropy in the country and has raised more than $30 million since 1977 for The Four Diamonds Fund.

being played in the far corner. The stockily built man with the salt-and-pepper crew cut on one side of the net, I would soon learn, was Nick Thiel. His partner was Gene Wettstone. The only other person in the building was John Lawther, shooting baskets on the middle court. I would wonder in later years how unusual it was that the first three persons I would see on campus were these three varsity coaches.

I exited Rec Hall but did not look to the left, where the recently installed Nittany Lion was crouching; instead, I moved on to the Tri-dorms area. As I walked through the quadrangle, I was surprised to see women's underwear strung on wash lines across the windows. A local custom, no doubt. Girls approached in groups of twos and threes, all dressed alike in barded shirts and dungarees, red handkerchiefs dangling from a hip pocket. This was my first glimpse of the Curtiss-Wright Cadettes. Apparently, this small-town boy had a lot to learn about Penn State life.

—ROBERT BARRON, CLASS OF '49

Your Sister's House

MYTH: *There are no sorority houses at Penn State because of an old Pennsylvania law defining a dwelling that housed a certain number of unrelated women as a brothel.*

FACT: *Sorority houses did exist on the University Park campus at one time, and there is neither any such state law nor a University prohibition against sorority houses. Chi Omega, established in 1926, was Penn State's first sorority, though the first sorority to occupy a house on campus was Kappa Alpha Theta. In 1928, Stone House (built in 1880 as the vice president's house; see page 3) became home to Nita-Nee, a women's social club that became KAΘ in 1930. The KAΘ sorority occupied the house until 1949. Other sororities also had campus houses but, like KAΘ, they moved out of these aging structures soon after World War II and into newly available suites in residence halls. The sororities then rented the suites from the University, as they do today. The advantages of residence hall suites and the high cost of private housing in the postwar era discouraged off-campus sorority houses, although the borough of State College's zoning laws make no distinction between sorority and fraternity houses.*

1O INFORMATION SCIENCES AND TECHNOLOGY BUILDING (2003)

Ironically, one of the most recent additions to Penn State has some of the oldest architectural roots of any building on campus. Rafael Viñoly, who designed the Information Sciences and Technology (IST) Building with Perfido Weikopf, modeled the steel, brick, and glass structure after the famous Ponte Vecchio. Just as the fourteenth-century Italian bridge spans Florence's Arno River, the eight-hundred-foot walkway of the IST Building extends over North Atherton Street, allowing pedestrians to move above the four-lane highway with ease. Indeed, the building caters to a large volume of foot traffic with several electronics retailers and a small café.

The IST Building is more than a convenient thoroughfare, though. The $60 million project was undertaken first and foremost as a center for interdisciplinary study in information sciences and technology, computer science, and engineering.

Contained within the building's three stories are the 160-seat Cybertorium, graduate student offices, and conventional classrooms and labs. But even the traditional spaces adhere to the structure's cutting-edge theme: the entire building is configured for wireless Internet access, meaning that any student with a laptop computer and the necessary hardware can access the Penn State network anywhere in the building.

The project was not without controversy as construction of the building progressed. Many students wrote letters to the *Daily Collegian* expressing concern about the hefty price tag, particularly in the face of rising tuition bills and diminishing state funding. Other area residents worried about the inconvenience of closing Atherton Street during the building's construction. University president Graham Spanier addressed such concerns on the *Daily Collegian*'s op-ed page, outlining both financial and philosophical reasons that such projects are necessary to the University's continued growth. Disagreements aside, now that the IST Building is complete, it is difficult to look up from the street at its gleaming arcs, or to look down from the walkway toward the cars streaming below, and not marvel at the achievement.

. . . . .

Where in the World Is the Water Tunnel?

What Penn State facility holds secrets yet exists in plain sight? The Garfield Thomas Water Tunnel, set diagonally across Atherton Street from Walker Building, was completed in 1949 under the auspices of the University's Ordnance Research Laboratory (now the Applied Research Laboratory, or ARL), largely sponsored by the U.S. Navy. The high-speed water tunnel, at one time the largest in the world, was built primarily to develop and test underwater weapons systems. More recently, it has served as a testing ground for experiments in fluid dynamics and acoustics. Research based on the tunnel—much of which remains classified—has contributed to our knowledge about systems above water, too, including artificial heart valves, car heating and cooling, and the workings of the space shuttle. Named for Penn State journalism graduate Lt. (j.g.) W. Garfield Thomas, who lost his life serving in World War II, the tunnel was completely overhauled in 1992 and remains a productive research base. Like the cable cars in San Francisco, the Apollo Command Module, the Johnstown Incline, and the Penn State Heart-Assist Pump, the Garfield Water Tunnel has been designated a Historic Mechanical Engineering Landmark by the American Society of Mechanical Engineers. But contrary to the decades-old legend, the Garfield Tunnel allegedly does not run under Atherton Street all the way to the Breazeale Nuclear Reactor. ("Well, how else would they be able to test submarines?")

ANY OF US WHO were fortunate enough during World War II to get in some of our schooling at Penn State before being drafted or volunteering for military service will recall that we had substantial numbers of military personnel taking classes and training on campus as part of programs like the Navy V-12 and the Army Specialized Training. Many may not recall that we also had two other rather unique, nonmilitary training groups on campus in the 1943–44 period.

These were the young ladies sent here by Hamilton-Standard Propeller and Curtiss-Wright to take engineering, math, and other technical training to prepare them to assume key positions with those firms in the all-out war effort. They didn't march to class like some of the military trainees, but they were no less recognizable with their arms loaded with slide rules and calculus texts. (No one then had yet heard of "book bags.")

11 LEONHARD BUILDING (1999) / EARTH AND ENGINEERING SCIENCES BUILDING (2000)

Leonhard Building, pictured here, was named after Penn State alumnus and philanthropist William Leonhard (Class of 1936). One of the more recent additions to the campus, the building houses the Department of Industrial and Manufacturing Engineering (College of Engineering), founded in 1908. Penn State's Industrial Engineering program has more laboratory space for student instruction and research than any other IE program in the country, and the three-story, 60,000-square-foot Leonhard Building illustrates the significance of hands-on learning. Leonhard's centerpiece is the Factory for Advanced Manufacturing Education (FAME) Laboratory, which provides students with learning experiences in a real manufacturing environment. The laboratory boasts state-of-the-art production technologies, including a computer-integrated manufacturing area and industrial material handling robots, as well as more traditional equipment. Catwalks on the upper floors allow classes to observe safely the manufacturing processes taking place below, which include casting, welding, assembly, and machining.

Visitors to the Leonhard Building will discover in its lobby an exact replica of the Liberty Bell—minus its famous crack—cast by the West

Philadelphia Bronze Company in 1996 to commemorate the establishment of the American Foundrymen's Society a century before. Also on display are a foot-powered lathe dating from 1876 and a collection of precision instruments from the Starrett and Lufkin companies. Across from Leonhard stands Earth and Engineering Sciences, a massive structure shared by the College of Engineering and the College of Earth and Mineral Sciences. EES houses classrooms and lecture halls as well as a number of offices, including those of the Department of Engineering Science and Mechanics and the Earth and Environmental Systems Institute.

· · · · ·

Rosie the Riveter Meets Ellen the Engineer

In 1942, Penn State became one of eight institutions to enter into a contract with the Curtiss-Wright Corporation, a manufacturer of aviation equipment, to train young women in fundamental engineering skills. Unable to find enough men to satisfy its demand for technically trained personnel, Curtiss-Wright sought to educate women in mechanical drawing, aerodynamics, foundry operations, and related subjects. The first class of 107 women began their all-expenses-paid, twenty-two-week course at Penn State in February 1943. They received a small stipend, too, in exchange for agreeing to use their new skills in Curtiss-Wright defense plants. The Cadettes were soon followed by groups of women from other

Most of these Cadettes (as they called themselves) were housed in McAllister Hall or Tri-dorms (Irvin, Watts, etc.). Their meals were provided in a dining area in the basement of Old Main. For their evening dinner they were required to dress appropriately, they sat at tables of ten, and the meal was served to them by a uniformed waiter. They were a positive and welcome addition to the campus in those days, although probably not adored by many coeds (men were in *very* short supply!). I dare say that many of these Cadettes treasured the experience and are probably great Penn State ambassadors to this day.

How do I know some of this? I was one of those very fortunate waiters who served them and got to know them.

—BILL McTURK, CLASS OF '48

aviation companies, notably the Hamilton-Standard Propeller Division of the United Aircraft Corporation, the Consolidated-Vultee Corporation, and the Glenn L. Martin Company.

Fraternity houses had been converted to barracks for military students, including men enrolled in the Navy's V-12 officer training program and the Armed Services Training Program. Women from the aviation companies were housed in the under-occupied men's residence halls, such as Watts and Jordan, and ate their meals at the Old Main Sandwich Shop. By the following year, with the end of the war still more than a year away, the government began reducing expenditures for training personnel on college campuses. The Curtiss-Wright Cadette class of 1944 was canceled.

WHEN I WAS PHOTO EDITOR of the *Daily Collegian* in the 1960s, I used to put in some late nights at the Sackett Building *Collegian* office. If my work was finished too late to go back to my apartment before my first class (which I learned to schedule no earlier than noon), I dragged three chairs into the darkroom, lined them up, and got a few hours of sleep. It was the perfect place to escape the light of dawn.

—KEN FRANKLIN, CLASS OF '65

I2 SACKETT BUILDING (1930; MAJOR RENOVATIONS 1951, 1958, 1979) / HAMMOND BUILDING (1960; RENOVATED 1977)

The College of Engineering, which was formally established in 1896, is housed in a collection of campus buildings that has grown over the years to include Sackett, Hammond, Electrical Engineering East and West, Leonhard, Earth and Engineering Sciences, Reber, Hallowell, and Fenske, among others. Its basic location on campus, however, has been generally fixed since 1893, when the Old Engineering Building—on the site where Sackett now stands—was dedicated under the approving gaze of University president George Atherton, Pennsylvania governor Robert Pattison, and U.S. Secretary of the Interior John Noble. With the exception of Old Main itself, Old Engineering was then the most costly building erected at Penn State.

Designed by Frederick Olds, the brick-and-sandstone Old Engineering was massive and dramatic, with an arched stone entrance, broad steps, and onion-domed turrets. It was impressive in its practicality as well, providing heat and electricity for the entire campus. Still, despite its size, its classroom conditions were crowded: some classes were held in hallways, and over the years engineering courses spread into a number of nearby units.

A devastating fire destroyed Old Engineering on November 25, 1918. Despite the efforts of firefighters from State College, Bellefonte, and Tyrone, the entire building burned out of control for hours. One witness wrote that it was "one of the worst fires I have ever looked at. . . . The main engineering building, containing the boilers, dynamos, wood room and machine shop has burned to the ground and all the college buildings are without heat and light." College representatives estimated the damage at $300,000.

The "new" main engineering building—the construction of which was begun a decade after the 1918 disaster—was finished in 1930 and eventually named after the former dean of the College of Engineering, Robert Sackett, who retired in 1937. Its red brick and limestone facade, shown opposite, complements the architectural style of several other campus buildings from the period, including Rec Hall. Along with classrooms and office space, Sackett houses the Department of Civil and Environmental Engineering and the College of Engineering's Environmental Institute.

Attached to Sackett is Hammond Building (right) built between 1958 and 1960 by Howell, Lewis, Shay and Associates. It was named for Harry Parker Hammond, dean of the College of Engineering from 1937 to 1951. (The State College station for the Bellefonte Central Rail Road—which provided service three times each day between State College and the county seat—stood on the site before Hammond was built.) Hammond now houses a number of research centers, such as the Rotorcraft Center of Excellence and the Center for Acoustics and Vibration, as well as the Department of Aerospace Engineering and the Engineering Library.

A HISTORICAL REFLECTION
THE ARCHITECTURE OF PENN STATE

CRAIG ZABEL

At the heart of Penn State's University Park campus stands Old Main. If you look closely you will find the words "Old Main" carved on its entablature, suggesting that this building dates back to the institution's origins in 1855. In fact, today's Old Main was built in 1929–30 to replace the original, crumbling Old Main. The first building, built in 1857–63 under the direction of Hugh N. McAllister, had housed essentially the entire institution at its beginning, when it was the Farmers' High School. This was typical of early college architecture in America; the first building of a college was usually a large structure much like an oversized house, with a central cupola or tower denoting its more institutional character.

While the original Old Main at Penn State once housed the classrooms, offices, chapel, and even dormitories and faculty housing for the College, the new Old Main was built to be a symbolic center that would house the central administration (and, at first, student activities) for an ever-expanding college campus. Its architect, Charles Z. Klauder, reused the rough gray limestone of the original building to erect a building with Federal revival detailing, a massive portico on an imperial scale, and a cupola reminiscent of New York City Hall, which had been constructed in the early nineteenth century. Although it did not have as many floors as the enormous hulk of the old structure, the new Old Main appears grander, more dignified and refined, befitting the growing importance of the institution.

In order to understand the architecture of Penn State, one must appreciate the university's rural location at the center of Pennsylvania. In the nineteenth century, new state colleges and universities were often intentionally located in bucolic, healthy surroundings, away from urban temptations so

I would like to extend my appreciation to the staff of the Penn State University Archives, Special Collections, University Libraries, for their assistance. Daniel Willis deserves my thanks for suggestions on a draft of this essay. I am also indebted to the scholarship of two of my former students, Laura Paris and Kurt Pitluga. For more information, consult the Selected Bibliography.

The original Old Main

that students could focus on their studies with no sinful distractions. Also, a central location within a state democratically implied ready access for all. Penn State's isolation, however, meant that it would continue to be a difficult location to reach well into the twentieth century. One early president declared that Penn State was "Equally Inaccessible from All Parts of the State." Nonetheless, Penn State grew on essentially an open and unfettered site in Centre County. The adjoining borough of State College was not even incorporated until 1896. Penn State's main campus developed as a series of widely spaced and coordinated groupings of buildings interspersed with impressive stands of trees and broad lawns (all very different from a congested urban campus).

Also important to our understanding of the early development of Penn State's architecture is its designation in 1863—when it was called the Agricultural College of Pennsylvania—as Pennsylvania's only land-grant institution. President Abraham Lincoln had signed the Morrill Land-Grant Act in 1862 to stimulate states to develop colleges and universities that would train students in the practical fields of agriculture, mechanical arts, and military tactics. In 1874, the College's name was changed to The Pennsylvania State College, and despite its major public mission as a land-grant institution, it remained a private corporation not owned by the state.

Many of the buildings erected during the late nineteenth and early twentieth centuries reflected these land-grant priorities. The mechanical arts were eventually served by an impressive new Engineering Building, completed in 1893. President George Atherton felt that placing a priority on training engineers in one of the most industrialized states in the nation made a great deal of sense. Frederick Olds, the architect of the Engineering Building, added two other structures on what was then a portion of Allen Street—and is now the campus Mall. His Armory Building (1888) helped fulfill the military mission that accompanied Penn State's land-grant status, while the Old Botany Building (1887) expanded the College's agricultural offerings. Unfortunately, of these three, only Old Botany still stands. (The Engineering Building fell in

Renovations to Old Main in the late nineteenth century

a catastrophic fire in 1918 and, in a low point for historic preservation, the Armory was demolished in 1964 to make way for one of Penn State's least likable classroom buildings, the Willard extension.) But with these three buildings, Olds was bringing to Penn State a more fashionable and sophisticated architecture reflective of the Romanesque revival of Henry Hobson Richardson. Olds's variation on the Richardsonian Romanesque stood in stark contrast to the ungainly mid-nineteenth-century bulk of the original Old Main. His brick and stone buildings looked as though they were built for the ages, with their picturesque massing, solid arches, and broad, enveloping roofs. One now only has Old Botany on the Mall to conjure up these ghosts of Penn State's earliest architecture.

At the turn of the twentieth century Penn State quickly moved away from the dark medievalism of Olds's Victorian architecture. The World's Columbian Exposition in Chicago in 1893 was a triumph for Beaux-Arts clas-

The Armory and Old Main

Construction of the "new"
Old Main, completed in 1930

sicism, and the ensuing City Beautiful movement shaped civic centers and college campuses across America. Coordinated ensembles of academically polished classical designs gave such locales as these their own incarnations of Chicago's White City. At Penn State, this trend began with the light beige classicized blocks and elegant Renaissance revival arches of Schwab Auditorium and the Carnegie Library's terra cotta classical motifs. (Schwab was built in 1902–3 and designed by Edward Hazlehurst; Carnegie, designed by Davis and Davis, was constructed in 1903–4.) These two buildings, funded by Charles M. Schwab and Andrew Carnegie—both of whom were on Penn State's Board of Trustees—reflect the growing importance of Penn State in the eyes of Pennsylvania's industrialists and such steel barons as Schwab and Carnegie. Large College functions could now take place in the spacious Schwab Auditorium rather than in the original Old Main's cramped chapel. And with Carnegie's construction, the library could move out of its inadequate quarters in Old Main to occupy its own structure, reflecting the growing liberal-arts initiatives in the College. (Carnegie remained the library's home until Pattee opened in 1940.)

Perhaps the most enchanting grouping of early Penn State buildings to survive into the twenty-first century is Ag Hill. Removed from the growing formality of the Mall, this cluster of buildings crowns a low hill north of Old Main and provided an early subcampus for agriculture within Penn State. The Philadelphia architect Edward Hazlehurst designed a Creamery (1903, now Patterson), the Main Agriculture Building (1905, now Armsby) and the Horticulture Building (1915, now Weaver). Informally wedged in between the Patterson and Armsby buildings stands the diminutive Calorimeter Building (1902), designed by Dean Henry Armsby for his early controlled experiments on the intake and "outtake" of cows. These four buildings are exemplars of the mason's craft, exhibiting fine proportions, subtle colors, and dignified massing. Their rectangular blocks are contained under broad, sweeping hipped roofs marking the landscape like Tuscan villas, while their masonry facades display an urbane gravitas. Simple Richardsonian Romanesque arches animate the Calorimeter Building, and the precise, tight brickwork of Patterson conveys a functional austerity. Armsby and Weaver are more sumptuous, with their complexly coursed walls and upper windows with Renaissance arches and engaged columns.

The architect who has had the greatest impact upon the architecture of Penn State's central campus is Charles Z. Klauder. The firm Day and Klauder of Philadelphia had begun to work on plans for Penn State in 1913. Frank Miles Day passed away in 1918, but Klauder continued to build and plan for Penn State up until his own death in 1938. Klauder was a prolific collegiate architect at many institutions across America, from Princeton University to the University of Colorado at Boulder. Perhaps his best-known (and most audacious) work is the Cathedral of Learning, built between 1924 and 1937 at the University of Pittsburgh. Klauder solidified his national reputation in collegiate architecture by co-authoring, with Herbert C. Wise, the book *College Architecture in America and Its Part in the Development of the Campus* (1929). It was Klauder who had the temerity to build the "new" Old Main (completed in 1930), erecting a

The Calorimeter Building (left, foreground) with Armsby (behind) and Patterson Building, once the College creamery (right)

West Halls

new and enhanced icon of Penn State's origins decades after the fact.

Klauder built in a variety of styles, and he believed that Georgian revival was appropriate for colleges desiring economy and order. (Collegiate Gothic could be much more expensive and thus was more appropriate for exclusive private colleges.) Much of what he designed for Penn State can be characterized as Georgian revival in style, leaning toward neoclassicism when greater monumentality was desired. One of Klauder's finest ensembles is West Halls (Jordan, Watts, and Irvin Halls, 1923–30). This U-shaped arrangement of residential halls suggests a picturesque grouping of Philadelphian Georgian row houses that are no longer contained by the city's streets but now grace a green terrace. West Halls is undergraduate living with dignity and class. The overall West Halls space is further embellished at the bottom of the slope, where the organizing axis terminates in the idiosyncratic bulge of the entrance rotunda of Klauder's Mineral Industries Building (constructed 1929–39, now Steidle Building).

The Steidle Building reflects Klauder's approach to many of the larger academic buildings he designed for Penn State. Large red brick Georgian revival blocks are ordered through strong cornices, pilasters accentuating end pavilions, and a monumental classical flourish at the main entrance. Klauder's use of Georgian and classical motifs can at times seem a touch unorthodox and mannered (a bit like his British contemporary Sir Edwin Lutyens). While Steidle is fronted with a conflation of a peristyle of columns, Roman attic, and Pantheon-like dome, a more common frontispiece for Klauder's buildings is a variation on a Roman triumphal arch, one that often idiosyncratically leaves out the central arch. An excellent example of this is the Henderson Building (built 1931–32). One enters such a building with a certain imperial gait (at least if one looks up at the Corinthian capitals and remembers one's architectural history class). Henderson was originally built as the Home Economics Building, and in the front lobby facing the entrance is a fireplace in a parlor-like setting, a shrine to the domestic hearth at the heart of the ideal 1930s American home. Another intriguing lobby can be found in Klauder's Sparks Building (built in stages between 1915 and 1938, and originally the Liberal Arts Building). Here, three Olympian-scaled benches have seats that are fronted with carved departmental names such as "Philosophy" and "History," carrying on an eternal, spectral faculty meeting amid the rushing and lounging students. Klauder even occasionally brought humor to his architecture. In designing a water tower topping a series of locker rooms (1936, now the Biomechanics Lab), he whimsically shaped it like a dome of a cathedral, complete with lantern, giving new arrivals to Penn State the distinct impression that there must be a Duomo here, rather than a more prosaic water tower. (This sleight of hand suggesting a Renaissance dome was later repeated on a second water tower at Penn State behind the Forum.)

Early on, Day and Klauder aspired to more than just red Georgian brick when they designed the Chemistry Building, elegantly sheathed in Indiana limestone (1917–30, now Pond Lab), one of the grander demonstrations of Beaux-Arts classicism at Penn State. But the City Beautiful memory of the 1893 White City would remain evoked primarily through the use of buff-colored brick (which began with Schwab and Carnegie), rather than stone, at Penn State's core. Red brick buildings would surround this central core. The beige brick core culminated in Klauder's most formal ensemble, the nearly identical Sparks and Burrowes (built 1937–38) buildings that flank Pattee Library. This U-shaped arrangement crowns the long sweep up from the corner of College Avenue and Allen Street and is reminiscent of Thomas Jefferson's design for the University of Virginia in Charlottesville (1817–26), with its library atop a terraced lawn leading down to a distant view of mountains. Rather than mimicking Jefferson's Pantheon-like rotunda, however, Klauder created a more abstract and cube-like composition for Penn State's library.

Pattee Library

Pattee Library (built 1937–40, designed by Klauder with Hunter and Caldwell) is one of Klauder's last works at Penn State. Its funding was assisted by the Public Works Administration, one of President Roosevelt's New Deal programs. Pattee reflects what one may call stripped classicism, a style that had become common by the 1930s, in attempts to modernize traditional compositions by making them more abstract. This style was also very appropriate for New Deal projects: it suggested that the United States was rebounding from the Great Depression by building for such central institutions as a college library a monumental structure that eschewed the decorative or ostentatious. Pattee almost takes on the character of "starved" classicism, though, on rainy days when one runs to get under the portico only to find that its mighty piers support no roof.

After World War II there was an immediate and acute need for student housing, which at first was expeditiously met with temporary trailers and barracks-like prefabricated buildings. As new permanent dormitories arose in the late 1940s, they remained stylistically conservative. Simmons, McElwain, Thompson, Hamilton, and McKee Halls (1947–50, designed by Harbeson, Hough, Livingston and Larson, or H2L2) all continued the Georgian revival style that Klauder had so well established, but without his subtlety or refinement. But postwar architecture in America was quickly embracing the International Style of modernism as promoted by Walter Gropius at Harvard University and Ludwig Mies van der Rohe at the Illinois Institute of Technology. When Pollock Halls (1958–60) arose behind Simmons and McElwain, a strong fissure between the traditional and the new was established, even though all of these dorms were by the same architects, H2L2 (the successor firm to the great Philadelphia architect Paul P. Cret). The genteel elegance and patina of earlier architectural traditions were replaced by an architecture of the contemporary, where stark multistoried high-rises efficiently housed hundreds of students. With the addition of H2L2's East Halls dormitory towers (1959–66), the east end of the University Park campus began to look like a partially realized fragment of Le Corbusier's utopian urban dreams of the 1920s: widely spaced, clean, machine-like blocks, which were now housing, feeding, and exercising thousands of students.

Penn State's rapid growth in the postwar era was also reflected in the institution's name, when The Pennsylvania State College became The Pennsylvania State University in 1953. Some buildings of enormous scale were built, such as the Hammond Building (built 1958–60, designed by Howell, Lewis, Shay and Associates) for engineering. This tall horizontal block in the International Style is clad in long ribbons of glass, thin salmon-colored panels, and an aluminum grid, like many of the skyscrapers and office parks of the period. The machine-like character of the upper walls contrasts with rough limestone at the building's base and end walls (an abstract tribute to the local limestone of Old Main that conversely reflects the later, more rustic aesthetics of Le Corbusier). Yet what has long disturbed many local residents about this building is its sheer bulk and monotony, as well as its lack of human scale and street-facing entrances. Two long blocks of Penn State's front yard to College Avenue and the State College borough are blocked by the blank stare of endlessly repeating machine-made modules. This is quite different from the noble sweep crowned by Klauder's monuments on the Mall and Old Main lawn just down College Avenue.

Most of the architectural design that was implemented at Penn State from the 1950s through the 1980s can be considered an institutional modernism that was functional but not overly distinguished or welcoming. Brick softened the rectilinear geometries of most of these buildings, and the choice of brick color was carefully coordinated to fit into the context of existing buildings. Some interesting groupings of buildings were created, such as the Arts Building with its Playhouse Theatre, the Music Building I with its Esber Recital Hall, and the Forum (1962–65, all designed by Eshbach, Pullinger, Stevens and Bruder). These buildings frame three sides of the Arts Court, now the Walter Walters Courtyard, complete with water fountain—Penn State's own modest reflection of the New York Lincoln Center for the Performing Arts, which was being built at that time.

An attempt to bring more adventurous architecture to Penn State occurred when Venturi and Rauch built the Faculty Club between 1974 and 1976 on a wooded lot between the Nittany Lion Inn and the College Heights neighborhood. A seminal figure in the development of postmodernism in architecture, the Philadelphia architect Robert Venturi had emerged in the 1960s and 1970s as one of America's most challenging architects and thinkers. The Faculty Club's tall shingled roof and broad eaves nestled into the context of the site, but the original function of the building was soon abandoned, and its playful and quirky original interior was unfortunately remodeled. (It is now the Executive Education Center.) When the Palmer Museum of Art underwent a major addition and transformation between 1990 and 1993, another pioneer of postmodernism, Charles W. Moore, was chosen as architect. Moore, with Arbonies King Vlock, rectified the blank modernist box of the original museum building (built 1967–72) by giving it a grand entrance. A stage-set-like curved arched loggia draws students past two disembodied bronze lion paws and into the museum. A growing

response to context and historical symbolism was being reintroduced to the Penn State campus.

The last fifteen years have seen a greater sensitivity to remodeling older buildings and to building new structures of quality and distinction. Splendid, human-oriented spaces that invite one to sit down and read Tolstoy or discuss Foucault have been added, such as the grandly traditional Paterno Family Humanities Reading Room, part of the remodeled Pattee Library (2000); the sweeping glazed pavilion of the convivial Café Laura in the Mateer Building (built 1991–93 and designed by John M. Kostecky Jr. and Associates); and the overstuffed comfort of the club-like Robb Hall on the first floor of the new Hintz Family Alumni Center (built 2000–2001 and designed by Purdy O'Gwynn Barnhart Architects). Internationally renowned architects are being commissioned to design "signature" buildings that often celebrate the latest in electronic technologies for major units of the university, such as Rafael Viñoly's sinuous, futurist bridge over Atherton Street for the Information Sciences and Technology Building (built 1999–2003, designed by Viñoly with Perfido Weikopf) and Robert A. M. Stern's Smeal College of Business Building with its soaring, proto-corporate atrium (built 2003–05, designed by Stern with Bower Lewis Thrower). Experimental structures are being built that are more environmentally responsible, as can be seen in the Stuckeman Family Building for the School of Architecture and Landscape Architecture (built 2003–05, designed by WTW/Overland), which was constructed according to strict national criteria for sustainable architecture to earn certification from the U.S. Green Building Council. This building will create a model of sustainability for future Penn State architecture. Georgian revival dormitories have even returned, now on a mammoth scale, with the new Eastview Terrace housing (built 2002–4, designed by Hayes Large/Childs Bertram Tseckares).

Perhaps the most striking change to the physical landscape of Penn State's University Park campus in recent years is the dramatic expansion of athletic facilities, culminating in the sixteen-thousand-seat Bryce Jordan Center (built 1993–96, designed by Haas/Rosser Fabrap/Brinjac, Kambic) and the most recent additions to Beaver Stadium (built 1999–2001, designed by John C. Haas Associates/HOK Sport). The towering open steel structure of this enormous football stadium looms over Penn State and dominates the landscape for miles. On six or seven Saturdays in the fall, Beaver Stadium truly becomes the central architectural landmark of the Penn State community: well over one hundred thousand people gather on its benches and in its luxury boxes for the much-anticipated home football games. In 2005, large-scale constructions continue to emerge across the campus as Penn State dynamically shapes its future physical environment in ways that will allow it to continue to evolve, reassess, and improve its educational, research, and service missions.

Pattee and Paterno Libraries

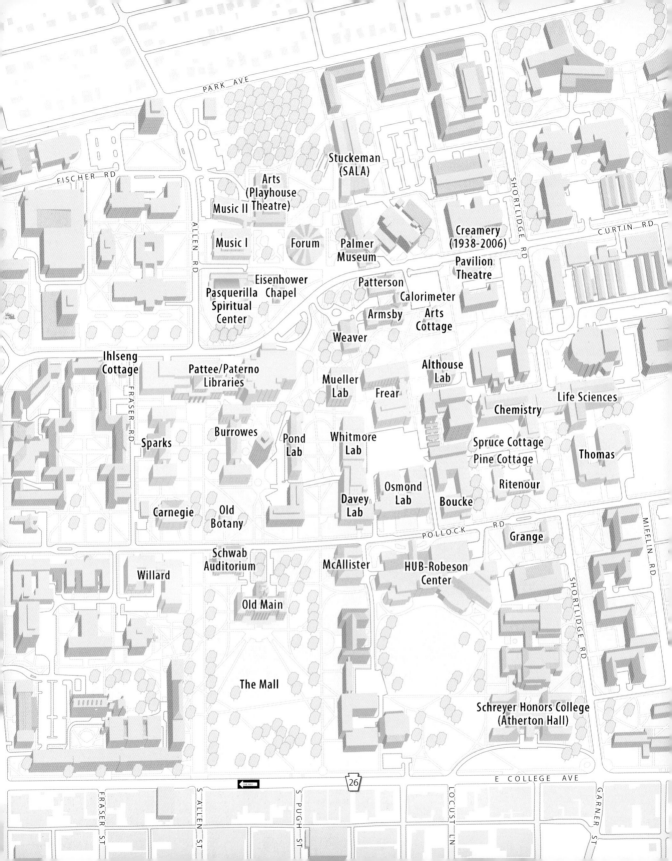

CENTRAL CAMPUS

The Mall · Old Main · Schwab Auditorium · Carnegie Building · Old Botany Building
Burrowes/Sparks Buildings · Pattee and Paterno Libraries · Pasquerilla Spiritual Center/Eisenhower Chapel
Music I/Music II/Arts Buildings · Stuckeman Family Building for the School of Architecture and Landscape Architecture
Palmer Museum of Art · The Creamery · Pavilion Theatre · Old Ag Hill Group
Life Sciences/Chemistry Buildings · Cottages · Eberly College of Science
HUB–Robeson Center · Student Services · Schreyer Honors College

I3 THE MALL

Penn State students frequent two local malls. The Nittany Mall, of course, provides "retail therapy." The other, greener Mall is a wide band of grass, flanked by walkways and trees, running from Pattee Library down to College Avenue. Several of the University's best-known buildings sit along the Mall, including Burrowes and Sparks at the north end, and Willard and Sackett farther south. Ask Penn State alums, however, and surely they will tell you that the single most distinctive feature of the Mall is its magnificent elm trees— among the longest standing rows of American elms anywhere in the world.

Not surprisingly, the elm trees, which are listed on the National Register of Historic Places, require almost constant maintenance. The oldest ones date back to the 1890s and are approaching the end of their life cycle; thanks to the University's "elm management plan," however, any elm lost to disease or severe weather is replaced with another American elm. Such care and attention to the elms is funded, in large part, by a gift from the Class of 1996. Summer and fall are lovely times of year to walk the Mall, when the elms' branches overhead create a dappled and leafy tunnel, as this picture shows.

During the warm months of the year, the Mall is a favorite spot for students, who often spend an afternoon reading or napping in the grassy center between its walkways. Those less studious or more energetic can be seen tossing a baseball or Frisbee back and forth or listening to the fire-and-brimstone pronouncements of the "Willard Preacher." But activity on the Mall is not always so leisurely. Heavy foot traffic, particularly near the concrete area directly in front of the Pattee steps, makes it a favorite place for gatherings of all kind—from political rallies to open-air performances of Shakespeare. And every July the Arts Festival sweeps in, bringing artists, craftspeople, and thousands of visitors from across the nation to Penn State and State College.

The Mall ends on the south side of campus at the Allen Street Gates. The present gates, from 1916, were based on an earlier set of gates from the St. Louis Expo of 1904. Like the northernmost part of the Mall, by the library, the Allen Street Gates are a lightning rod for social activism, attracting petition campaigns, memorials for fallen soldiers, peace vigils, "Honk for Hemp" and other political demonstrations, and fund-raising drives of all sorts.

·   ·   ·   ·   ·

Humble Squirrel Beginnings

The Pennsylvania State College
School of Education
Department of Nature Study, State College, PA

March 20, 1925

Miss Pauline Chapman, Treasurer
Women's Student Government Association
State House
State College, Pennsylvania

My dear Miss Chapman:

Yesterday Mr. H. C. Berkardt brought a check from your association for $30.00 . . . with which to purchase gray squirrels to be planted on our campus. Mr. Berkardt was under the impression that these creatures would be secured at $6.00 per pair and that the fund would secure five pairs. This information, however, is incorrect. The lowest price that I have been able to secure on these animals is $8.00 per pair. In order to secure four pairs of gray squirrels, the writer has added to this fund $2.00. . . .

I have advised President Thomas of your splendid contribution and have advised him that four pairs of squirrels have been ordered. Let me take this opportunity to thank your organization for fostering this splendid project. I am sure that the squirrels will find congenial surroundings on our campus and that in time they will multiply and become one of the interests and charms of our campus.

Very truly yours,
G. P. Green
Professor of Nature Study

· · · · ·

The Obelisk Complex

The Obelisk (or polylith, as it was originally called) was built in 1896 by State College stonemason Michael Womer as a symbol of the history of the College of Earth and Mineral Sciences. It contains 281 examples of Pennsylvania building stones—arranged in order of their geologic chronology. Climbing it was once the midnight initiation for Outing Club rock climbers. And despite the statement in a 1985 Harrisburg Patriot article that "good geologists know nothing about Freudian symbolism," psycho-geological legends surrounding this thirty-three-foot monument have long circulated among students. The most enduring one originated after World War II and claims that a virtuous coed's passing by will cause it to crumble. Interestingly enough, despite the comings and goings of well over one hundred classes of students, the Obelisk—the oldest monument on the University Park campus—remains structurally sound.

I STARTED PENN STATE in 1966, the same year that Joe Paterno was named head coach. My experience at PSU coincided with tumultuous times and rapid changes in University life. I recall as a freshman having to wear dresses and hose in order to gain admittance to Sunday dinner in the dining halls. By the time of my graduation, jeans and tie-dyed T-shirts were in vogue. Shortly after leaving Penn State, I relocated to Huntington Beach, California, where I still reside some thirty-four years later. In the early years, my only connection to the University was the occasional football game I could catch on TV and the annual Christmas cards exchanged with lifelong friends established at PSU.

The advent of the Internet has significantly strengthened and increased my Penn State connections and fervor. In 2000, despite living about 2,500 miles from State College, I arranged a reunion of my Alpha Delta Pi sorority sisters in Happy Valley. It was exciting to see folks that I had neither seen nor heard from for as long as thirty years. It renewed many connections previously lost.

In the past few years, I have developed even more Penn State

14 OLD MAIN (1863; RENOVATED LATE 1880S; RAZED 1929; NEW OLD MAIN COMPLETED IN 1930)

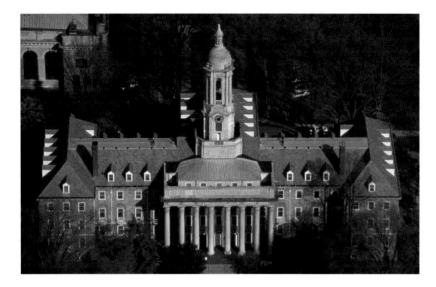

With new buildings appearing on campus almost every year and the physical boundaries of the University creeping ever outward, it is easy to forget that in its original incarnation, all of Penn State fit inside a single building. Farmers' High School accepted its first class in 1859, but it was not until late 1863 that construction on the College Building (later to be called Old Main) was completed. Designed by trustee Hugh N. McAllister, along with Frederick Watts and James Miles, "old" Old Main contained every element of daily life: offices, faculty and student living quarters, the dining hall, classrooms, and the entire library, shown on page 60 in a photograph from 1894. "Old Main Rats"—as students referred to themselves—and their instructors studied, ate, and slept all within the same walls. A fire in 1892 destroyed the building's roof, and although a series of repairs was made over the years, it eventually became apparent that Old Main had grown too small and too dilapidated to meet the school's needs. It was razed in 1929.

The new Old Main, completed in 1930, made use of much of the limestone from the old Main Building structure—limestone that was originally mined from the Old Quarry, a few hundred yards from where Old Main sits. With the expansion of the campus in the intervening years, it was no longer necessary to make Old Main a self-contained scholastic environment, but

ties through my love of Penn State football. One particular message board that I frequent, at www.nittanyfootball.com, has led to my developing new friendships that exist in cyberspace as well as real time. Members share our Penn State experiences, our passion for Penn State football, our politics, and our lives in a community that keeps growing and evolving. In 2003, we were able to make a contribution to the State College food bank through our Internet connections that brought pledges from several states. The most amazing thing about this new community is the fact that the originator of the board and many of its members are not even Penn Staters, but share the love of our University through football. If this is not an indication that the "Grand Experiment" is a success, nothing is.

My hope is to continue to strengthen my Penn State ties. In June 2005, after I retire, one of my first goals is to spend fall Saturdays with many of my old and new friends, cheering my alma mater on to victory. After all, WE ARE!

—CAROL BURKHOLDER PILGRIM,
CLASS OF '70

IN 1951, WHEN I STOOD "at child-hood's gate / Shapeless in the hands of fate," I saw a renovated bathhouse, not stately Old Main. I have many fond memories of the University Park campus, but my life-long love affair with Penn State began and remains at the Altoona Undergraduate Center (a.k.a. Penn State Altoona).

Although Penn State Altoona has been touted as the "Flagship of the Commonwealth Campuses," there was a time when it wouldn't have qualified as a dinghy. In the late 1940s, the Undergraduate Center decided to build a campus on the abandoned Ivyside Park amusement park site. Classes were held in a ren-ovated bathhouse and the refur-bished skating rink served as the Student Union. The shooting gallery was converted into the chemistry lab. A bowling alley, left over from amusement park days, was put into use from time to time. At Ivyside Park, the only ivy was of the poison variety.

During my time there, every day was an adventure. There might be a skunk under the zoology lab, a skele-ton in the women's restroom ("bor-rowed" from the anatomy lab), or a heating or power failure. Office hours

architect Charles Z. Klauder still envisioned a building that would meet a vari-ety of needs. The new Old Main was intended not only to house the offices of the College president and various high-level administrators but also to pro-vide space for student organizations (including the offices of the *Daily Colle-gian*) and to serve as the student union. Not surprisingly, Old Main became a symbol of the University as a whole, as the lavish cake (above) celebrating Penn State's centennial shows.

But the College's rapid growth quickly made Old Main's diversity of pur-pose impossible. Administrative offices soon occupied most of the building's space. Even the Alumni Association, which for many years maintained its office in Old Main, eventually moved to the newly completed Hintz Family Alumni Center in 2001.

Old Main regularly announces its presence from the clock tower pic-tured here. In 1930, a half-ton bell was installed and rung on the hour. By 1937, though, it fell silent in favor of an electromagnetic recording and eight large speakers. The playback system has undergone numerous upgrades since then. The most recent was in 1993, when the quarter-hourly chime began to be played by a synthesizer weighing less than two pounds. On Fri-days, the tower rings the chorus to the Penn State fight song, "The Nittany

Lion." The other six days of the week, from the clock tower comes the West-minster Quarters, the familiar four-bar chime associated with clock towers all over the world.

. . . . .

"We Don't Know the Gosh-Darned Words"

With lyrics by Fred Lewis Pattee, Penn State's alma mater was proclaimed the official song of Penn State by former governor James A. Beaver in 1901. During his life, Pattee wrestled with the male-oriented language of his time, but it was not until 1975 that his original "When we stood at boyhood's gate" and "Thou didst mold us into men" were changed to their current form. To hear a more colorful alma mater lyric sung, attend any Penn State home football game and sit near the student section.

The Penn State Alma Mater

For the glory of old State,
For her founders strong and great,
For the future that we wait,
Raise the song, raise the song.

Sing our love and loyalty,
Sing our hopes that, bright and free,
Rest, O Mother dear, with thee,
All with thee, all with thee.

When we stood at childhood's gate,
Shapeless in the hands of fate,
Thou didst mold us, dear old State,
Dear old State, dear old State.

May no act of ours bring shame
To one heart that loves thy name,
May our lives but swell thy fame,
Dear old State, dear old State.

were anytime the instructor wasn't teaching. Students and instructors ate together in the Student Union. One student might be discussing baseball with the art instructor, another could be playing ping-pong with his history teacher, and someone else might be borrowing a dollar for lunch from the dean of students.

There are so many memories: Clean Up Day (a day set aside each semester to clean up the campus), the Friday night parties at the Student Union and the more formal dances at various places around the city, and all of the other activities. There were no upperclassmen, so we had to establish our own traditions. One that seems to be maintained is the spirit of friendliness that still pervades the Altoona campus.

When I return to Altoona, I always make a pilgrimage to the campus and marvel at how "Bathhouse U" has turned into a real college. I wouldn't trade anything (including the destruction of my first semester's transcript) for the experiences I had at the Altoona Undergraduate Center from 1951 to 1953.

—JOHN E. BOYD, CLASS OF '55

Penn State Alfresco

Covering more than 1,200 square feet, the Land-Grant Frescoes, which graciously span
the upper walls of the Old Main lobby, were completed in June 1949. Among the largest
works of their kind at any university, they portray the changes to American education
made possible by the passage of the Morrill Land-Grant Act in 1862.

In the early 1930s, Harold E. Dickson, J. Burn Helme, and Francis E. Hyslop—
professors of art and architectural history—conceived an idea for a mural that depicted
Penn State's founding and growth. Well-known fresco master Henry Varnum Poor, pictured opposite, was engaged in 1939 to create the work, thanks to the alumni gift of the
Class of 1932. After much preparation, Poor began painting the murals in April 1940.
Each morning his daughter Anne applied fresh plaster to the walls, with Poor painting
directly onto it, in true fresco technique. The north wall of the Old Main lobby staircase
was completed on June 18, 1940.

In December 1941, the sophomore, junior, and senior classes voted to provide funds
to continue the frescoes along the east and west walls, but World War II intervened and

the work was postponed. Poor finally returned to Old Main in 1948 to create new frescoes symbolizing the university's postwar relationship with the Commonwealth and its academic and community development. Completed in June 1949, the newer portions were also funded by postwar students and symbolized Penn State's postwar academic and extracurricular activities and services to the Commonwealth.

15 SCHWAB AUDITORIUM (1903)

> *The building from the first stirred the soul of Dr. Atherton as nothing else had done during his administration.*
>
> —Fred Lewis Pattee

Schwab Auditorium, with its Renaissance-style seating area and richly curtained stage, stands as a tribute to the power and importance of private donations to public institutions.

Charles M. Schwab, founder of the Bethlehem Steel Corporation, served as a member of the College's Board of Trustees between 1902 and 1932. In 1902, he donated more than $150,000 toward a new building to replace the seriously overburdened Old Main chapel. (Chapel attendance at that time was

IN THE SPRING OF my junior year, 1978, I was living in Hiester Hall in the Pollock quad. We were informed that there would be a dorm shortage for the next school year and anyone wanting to live on campus was going to have to win a room assignment in a dormitory lottery. Everyone else would have to find off-campus housing. My friends panicked and found apartments. For whatever reason— that sweet state of denial that comes with college life?—I chose to take my chances. The dorm application read "First choice?" I said, "Why not go for it all?" and checked off "West Halls." To live in West Halls meant I could just roll out of bed and stumble across the street to class. I was an English major and most of my classes were in Willard Building. Much to my amazement and my friends' envy, I not only got a dorm assignment but my room was in Thompson Hall. I couldn't have been closer to Willard. That set the stage for an incredible senior year. I spent as little time as possible "commuting to class," leaving the rest of my time available for more creative pursuits.

Living in West Halls meant that the Mall, which I could see from my window, became part of my everyday life. I realized it was more than just a wide sidewalk with gorgeous trees and manic squirrels; it was the major artery to College Avenue—

still mandatory.) Although glad for the generous gift, College president George Atherton predicted that the building would be used for a wide variety of events, and so argued against naming it Schwab Chapel, favoring instead the broader term "auditorium." Atherton envisioned the auditorium as an architectural masterwork, and he was so eager to get the building finished in time for 1903's commencement exercises that he ordered the construction site covered with a wooden shell and outfitted with heat and light so that the builders could work straight through the harsh winter weather. Atherton's persistence paid off, and in June 1903, students met for graduation in Schwab Auditorium, the first structure on campus built from private money.

A decade after the auditorium was completed, the gift of the Class of 1914 added a pipe organ, replaced in 1936 by that year's graduating class. Schwab's interior was renovated in 1999 with the installation of new carpets, drapes, and seats, and in 1947 its seating capacity had been slightly reduced (to 1,200) in order to comply with state regulations. Yet its basic architecture has remained unchanged since its opening more than a hundred years ago. Constant, too, have been some of the happenings on the auditorium's stage: the Penn State Thespians, a student-run musical theatre company and the University's oldest performance group, have called Schwab home since its completion in 1903. The auditorium also holds lecture classes too large for normal classrooms and plays host to visiting musicians and theatre troupes throughout the year. Guest artists at Schwab have included the late Spalding Gray, the Juilliard String Quartet, and the Los Angeles Guitar Quartet.

May He Rest in Penn State

George Atherton, Penn State's president from 1882 until his death in 1906, is often called Penn State's "second founder." Before he arrived, the school was in financial and curricular disarray and under investigation by legislators. Atherton—known to wear a skullcap in private to keep his bald head warm—was an outspoken, authoritative advocate for land-grant education. A drafter of the Hatch Act (1887) and the second Morrill Act (1890), which established federal aid to higher education, he charted a new course for Penn State, convincing lawmakers to support the school, adding new college buildings, and creating a coherent curriculum. Like many presidents since, Atherton often wrestled with Pennsylvania legislators over state appropriations and was known to use creative methods (including outright shame) to achieve his ends.

Paradoxically, Atherton had a reputation among students as both a revered administrator and a strict enforcer of the disciplinary code. He persuaded the Board of Trustees to remove its ban on fraternities in 1888, shortened the academic year in 1892, and tolerated the popular student "scraps"—encounters between large groups of freshmen and sophomores that, while a time-honored American college initiation tradition dating to colonial times, sometimes resulted in injuries and vandalism. In 1889, Atherton himself caused a student uprising by suspending Charles "Calamity" Musser, a sophomore who returned late from a brief Memorial Day vacation. Musser had a good excuse—the Johnstown Flood—but since news of the disaster had not yet reached Penn State, Atherton suspended him. Musser's fellow sophomores protested the unfair treatment by taking up residence, as the image here shows, in perhaps the first "tent city" in the fields west of campus, which they called "Camp Suspension."

east to the Waffle Shop and Sunday morning brunches and west to Le Bistro and those French '75s! The Mall is forever identified with the Preacher in front of Willard and Greek events at the College Avenue entrance. But far more happened there. It was the site of both celebration, like when Oklahoma lost (to Nebraska, I believe), assuring us a good bowl berth (we were undefeated that year!), and demonstration, like the line of silent, white-masked Iranian students protesting the Shah's rule at home.

Beyond the beauty and the convenience lies another reason for my feelings for the Mall. It was the arterial line to my boyfriend (now husband)—he worked at the Phyrst and lived right off Allen Street. We would often meet on the Mall to go somewhere together. Now whenever I go back to State College, I make a point of walking the Mall. I'm amused to see the little locks on the grates over the heating vent tunnels, meant to keep out the curious (let me just say they weren't there in 1979). But the Obelisk still stands, and the kids still walk to class and back home, and maybe the architecture students even hang out of the windows in the spring. Some things never change.

—THERESE D. BOYD, CLASS OF '79

Atherton's gravesite, also pictured here, is adjacent to Schwab Auditorium. In 1906, before Pollock Road became a major campus artery, this site seemed more tranquil to the Atherton family than the other proposed location—in front of Old Main.

16 CARNEGIE BUILDING (1904; RENOVATED 1941, 1962)

Carnegie Building—which has also been known as Carnegie Hall and Carnegie Library—was Penn State's first stand-alone library. It replaced the original two-room library located in Old Main (a space that had, by the late nineteenth century, become simply too limited for the library's nine thousand volumes). Designed by Seymour and Paul Davis and modeled after a library at Oxford University, Carnegie Building was presented on November 18, 1904, by steel magnate Andrew Carnegie. The presentation was festive, with performances by the College Orchestra and Glee Club and addresses by notables, including the governor of Pennsylvania, Samuel Pennypacker; Thomas Lynch Montgomery, the state librarian of Pennsylvania; George Atherton, the president of the College; and Carnegie himself. Carnegie had visited the College some years before, and he marked its progress, saying,

> It is twenty years since I was here and I feel like Rip Van Winkle, after he had slept twenty years. . . . This farmers' high school, I find, has now nineteen courses, embracing all subjects of human knowledge. Twenty

years ago I found 170 students here. To-day there are between 700 and 800 and the cry is "still they come."

The Carnegie Library had carefully prescribed rules. Some staff in 1915 were concerned with "the question of 'visiting' between the sexes," but ultimately decided that their main goal was to maintain quiet in the library, not to segregate men and women. And unlike today's undergraduates, who can borrow a hundred items at a time from the University Libraries—and keep them for nearly a month—patrons of the Carnegie Library could take out only two books at one time, and the volumes were due back to the library very quickly. (Department heads had more leeway: they could take out books for a full two weeks!)

When the library functions were moved to Pattee in 1941, Carnegie Building was adapted for classroom space for the music school and later became a center for student publications, including the *Daily Collegian* for much of its history. Since 1950, it has been home to the School of Journalism, now the College of Communications. The College boasts thirteen laboratories that offer students a chance to use state-of-the-art equipment in order to learn skills such as animation, media effects, digital and analog editing, and news writing.

I HAVE TWO fond humorous stories about college life.

I will never forget attending my first official function as an undergraduate student. I was a thirty-seven-year-old Navy veteran enrolled at Penn State University as a full-time freshman beginning in the fall term of 1969. Freshman orientation was scheduled at 6:00 P.M. in Schwab Auditorium. Having served over twenty years in the U.S. Navy, I was accustomed to arriving early at any lecture and sitting in the front row. Soon 6:00 P.M. arrived, no presenter; 6:15 P.M., same thing. At 6:30 P.M. several other freshman students approached me and said, "Sir, we have been waiting for one half hour; when are you going to start with the orientation?" My reply, much to their astonishment, was "I am a freshman student also." The expressions on their faces were priceless. Shortly afterward, a staff member from the admissions office arrived and apologized for the unexpected delay. Those students and I had a good laugh. At the time, I didn't think that I looked that old and distinguished, but I was delighted to be mistaken for a Penn State University staff member.

My second humorous experience as an undergraduate student at Penn State involved my daughter Marcia Werba McShane (Classes of '75 and '80) and me. I was a forty-year-old senior and she was an eighteen-year-old freshman. I saved one elective course so that we could have one class together during our

Scrap Happy

Before Beaver Canyon and bar tours, the "scraps" or "rushes" of the late nineteenth and early twentieth centuries initiated many freshmen into college life. A scrap, according to University historian Michael Bezilla, "was a good natured but often brutal encounter between large numbers of freshmen and sophomores," organized to build class loyalty. Injuries and property damage were not uncommon. Very often students gathered in the large fields behind the Armory, as shown above (notice the Obelisk in the distance), sometimes at pre-arranged times. (More than occasionally they met spontaneously, when the spirit moved them.) Scraps took many forms, and they included both "official" participants and an enthusiastic audience, often ending with a bonfire fueled by whatever was gathered by the frenzied mob.

The object of the "cane rush" was to see who could get the most hands on a cane, freshmen or sophomores. Needless to say, with the crowd rather large and the cane quite small, many flailing limbs were pulled and crushed in the ensuing melee. The flag scrap was similar, with members of each class attempting to seize a flag from the top of a flagpole while simultaneously beating back opponents from the other class. During a pants scrap of 1924—pictured opposite—sophomores literally tore the pants off freshmen, sometimes to the point of embarrassment. At the annual picture scrap, freshmen attempted to assemble for a class photo without the knowledge of sophomores, whose "duty" it was to disrupt the portrait. Once the secret location of the frosh portrait was revealed, an alarm sounded and sophomore students left their classrooms to rush to the scene, using any and all means possible to keep the photo from being taken. Often the photographer was just as injured as the scrappers.

With the advent of indoor plumbing, student-instigated outhouse bonfires became somewhat popular with State College residents, who were saved the expense of removing their Crappers when gangs of students carted them away. But as the number of injuries and the cost in property damages increased, college and borough officials became less likely to overlook scraps, rushes, and bonfires as good, clean college fun. In one incident, a freshman fled a sophomore "molasses and sawdust" mob and barricaded himself in a State College boarding house. The pursuing horde filled a cadet corps cannon with vegetables stolen from local gardens and fired it at the house, breaking nearly all of the windows. In September 1907, one student even died from injuries sustained at a freshman-sophomore brawl in which five hundred students participated.

By 1916, most scraps were officially abolished by the student body and an attempt was made in the 1920s to replace them permanently with other events, such as poster night and stunt night. Even those activities sometimes resulted in molasses-and-feathers-coated freshmen and bruises and broken bones, however, and vandalism continued. Under pressure from college administrators, the Student Council instituted a series of less physical activities, which aroused little student interest. Commenting on such lackluster events, the Collegian warned that school spirit was diminishing as the student "he-men" of yesteryear were being replaced by the "lounge lizards" and "cake-eaters" of current days. Some alumni even campaigned to restore the bone-crushing scraps of the Atherton era. But what few scraps remained faded away by the 1930s, replaced over time by a socially enforced dress code. Freshmen males complied by wearing green "dinks," or beanies, and following the rules written on "Freshmen Proclamation" posters plastered throughout campus. Any violators of these customs could receive from his fellow students a block "S" haircut or—you guessed it—the molasses and feather treatment.

college experience at Penn State. We were enrolled in Chemistry 11 and voluntarily signed up as laboratory partners. Nobody knew at the time that we were father and daughter. In the laboratory, we were involved in an experiment using the Mettler balance to determine the weight of an unknown mass. Apparently, while we were working together, I must have been really vocal and assertive during the experiment, to the extent that it was noticed by some of the other students in the lab. Marcia, in my opinion, was not following directions properly and I, as a dutiful father, was doing my best to correct her. Some students informed the professor. He approached us at our station and inquired if I had some type of a problem working with my lab partner. I replied that I had no problem working with this individual and had been dealing with minor problems with her for quite some time. He frowned, looked at me, and then at Marcia. I felt that this was the appropriate time to relieve the tension. I asked Marcia, "Please tell the professor what you call me." She replied, "Dad." A smile crossed the professor's face and we could feel the tension disappear. During this conversation, the students in the immediate vicinity were watching and listening intently. When everyone found out that we were father and daughter, smiles were the order of the day.

—ROBERT G. WERBA, CLASS OF '72

17 OLD BOTANY BUILDING (1887)

Old Botany Building is the oldest academic building on campus whose exterior has not undergone significant renovation. It was designed by Frederick Olds in the Romanesque revival style of Henry Hobson Richardson, a style that Olds also used for Old Engineering and the Armory. Old Botany's most notable features are the large semicircular window on its east facade, eyelid dormers, and terra cotta ornamentation on the ridge of the roof.

While Old Botany has been a constant for well over a century, its surroundings have been anything but. The structure was designed to house botany laboratories, but a glass conservatory (featuring stained glass in the entryway and elaborate ironwork) was soon erected alongside the building. Students laid out impressive formal gardens in the front, while parallel lines of spruce and pine trees, dubbed the "Ghost Walk," stood nearby. Eventually, additional greenhouses and a small powerhouse stretched behind Old Botany. Photographs from the 1890s and early 1900s show students in the greenhouses examining tropical plants—a feat possible in central Pennsylvania's winter chill only thanks to the dedicated powerhouse.

By 1939, the Department of Botany had moved to new offices on campus, and the greenhouses had been dismantled. But Old Botany continued to serve as a home for smaller academic departments and programs. Today,

Penn State's Science, Technology, and Society program calls ivy-covered Old Botany home.

Campus legend holds that spirits haunt the area around Old Botany. (Such tales even appeared in the *Daily Collegian* as far back as 1928.) One ghost—that of Frances Atherton, widow of former Penn State president George Atherton—allegedly peers out of the attic's front windows, keeping watch over her husband's grave outside Schwab Auditorium.

18 BURROWES BUILDING (1938; RENOVATED 1967) / SPARKS BUILDING (1915; ADDITIONS BUILT BY 1938)

Burrowes and Sparks buildings, twin complements to Pattee Library, both feature the neoclassical design favored by Charles Z. Klauder, architect of numerous other buildings on the campus. Inside Burrowes, facing murals by John Thomas Biggers—*Night of the Poor* and *Day of the Harvest*—adorn the foyer. Both were painted in 1947, while Biggers was a Penn State student. (Biggers's other major work of this period, his *Sharecropper Mural*, is displayed in the Robeson Center.)

Burrowes Building, pictured here, was built for the School of Education and named for Thomas Henry Burrowes, president of the College from 1868 to 1871. Burrowes was dedicated to public education, and—along with other educational pioneers—he helped establish public schools as well as the system of normal schools in Pennsylvania, today's Pennsylvania State System of Higher Education. When his namesake building was erected, the dean of the School of Education asked Carroll Champlin, a professor of the history of education, to select names to be engraved in the frieze at the top of the building. Champlin's list included legislators, philosophers, college presidents, psychologists, and commissioners and other leaders in the field of education. Some of the names have been obscured by the wings added to Burrowes in the late 1960s, but they include Erasmus, Montaigne, Rousseau, William James, C. Stanley Hall, Thomas Huxley—and the lone woman on the list, Anna Comstock, a professor at Cornell University from 1913 to 1920 who advocated "nature education."

Like Burrowes, Sparks Building also features a frieze with the names of celebrated thinkers and authors—eighty-four in all. Dean Charles Stoddart asked the faculty of the liberal arts for a list of "men . . . rated as the world's greatest characters," and Stoddart compiled the list after receiving names from the faculty. These "characters" range from Benjamin Rush, Hawthorne, Whitman, Abraham Lincoln, and George Washington to Samuel Clemens, Voltaire, Confucius, Goethe, Aristotle, Cervantes, Tolstoy, Tennyson, Galileo, and Dickens. (One woman made this list, too: Mary Lyon, the founder of Mount Holyoke College, who made a lasting impact on higher education by insisting on expanded academic opportunities for women.)

Today, Burrowes provides space for the Departments of English and Comparative Literature as well as departments and programs dedicated to foreign language study. Sparks holds the administrative offices of the College of the Liberal Arts as well as the Departments of Communication Arts and Sciences, Philosophy, and Linguistics.

· · · · ·

"Accuracy. Fairness. Balance. Presence."

These, in the words of one former editor in chief, explain the phenomenal success of the Daily Collegian, Penn State's student newspaper. Indeed, the paper has come a long way from its origins as the Free Lance, a monthly publication that hit the streets of State College in April 1887. The Bellefonte Central train brought copies of the Free Lance to town that spring, and an impromptu march down College Avenue ensued as students hailed the arrival of the first issue—twelve pages, bound in blue, and selling for fifteen cents.

The Free Lance was Penn State's first official student newspaper, and it featured news and commentary on current events at the College and in the world at large, as well as occasional literary endeavors. It noted the arrival of Penn State's first fraternity, reported the sporting news, pondered the question of coeducation—eventually deciding that a woman's education should simply "make her queen of the household and society" and that too much study would make women "permanent invalids"—and editorialized in support of Prohibition. In 1904, the State Collegian succeeded the Free Lance (which had, some years before, become a largely literary enterprise). Seven years later, the renamed Penn State Collegian began semiweekly publication, and in the fall of 1940, the newspaper became the Daily Collegian.

The paper has covered everything from the decisions of Penn State's presidents and the University's relationship with Harrisburg to student demonstrations and protests, national crises such as the Kennedy assassination and the terrorist attacks of September 11, 2001, tuition hikes, the nation's and campus's struggles for racial and gender equality, and, of course, sports. The award-winning Daily Collegian now ranks alongside many small-city daily newspapers in its coverage of international and national events. And as of 1996, it could also boast an online presence—as the Digital Collegian.

19 PATTEE LIBRARY (1940; ADDITIONS 1953, 1966, 1972) / PATERNO LIBRARY (2000)

Penn State's library was born with a modest donation of fourteen books in 1857. By the time a space was set aside for a library in Old Main, the collection consisted of almost 1,500 volumes in agriculture and the sciences. Today's Pattee and Paterno Libraries provide more than 490,000 square feet of space for the University Libraries' growing collection of more than 4.7 million volumes, and they serve more than 84,000 students across the state.

Penn State's first librarian, Professor William Buckhout, was appointed in 1874 and allowed students supervised access to the books for one hour per day. It was not until 1888 that library hours were extended to six hours a day. Helen Bradley became the first female librarian in 1895, and she extended services and expanded the subject collections until, by the turn of the century, severe overcrowding led to the construction of the Carnegie Library in 1903–4. By the 1930s, even Carnegie was too small, and Pattee Library was built between 1937 and 1940 as part of a multi-building Public

"BACK THEN" you did not visit the colleges that you hoped to enter, you sent letters. Hence, most often your introduction to your place of occupation for the next four years was when you arrived with luggage. My choice of major was Chemical Engineering. Dean Whitmore taught a class the first semester for freshmen and one the last semester for seniors. His first words gave most of us quite a start when he casually asked us to look to the left and then to the right and commented that probably you or they would be missing at the end of the first year! It was true—and the mayhem did not end then. Addressing a much, much smaller senior class, he started by telling us what we all knew—that jobs were very difficult to get. He said that his course would be on the preparation of a letter of application, and then he said that everyone who was in the class could get a job if they wrote enough letters. Most of us wrote considerably over a hundred letters.

We had two electives that first year and, having some interest in music, I made a request to the head of the Music School for an elective course. His response, emphatic beyond belief, was that anyone in

Works Administration–General State Authority project. Over the next three decades, three major additions to Pattee appeared: the 1953 Stack Building, West Pattee in 1966, and East Pattee in 1972.

Construction began on the Paterno Library in the spring of 1997 and was completed in September 2000. Coach Joe Paterno led the library's fund-raising campaign, stating with characteristic candor, "You can't have a great university without a great library." The campaign also financed renovations to Pattee Library, including its east entrance and sculpture, pictured on page 73. Don't miss the Paterno Family Humanities Reading Room on the second floor, which is modeled after historic library reading rooms but is also "wired" for contemporary patrons, with its green-shaded reading lamps housing data ports.

Just inside the renovated Mall entrance of Pattee Library, beyond the steps and square columns shown here, resides the "original" Nittany Lion— the only known mounted specimen of an eastern mountain lion, which had become Penn State's mascot by 1907. It was killed in Susquehanna County by Samuel Brush (hence its additional moniker of "Brush Lion") in 1856, just one year after the University was established as the Farmers' High School. A fierce creature indeed, as visitors can testify! A touch-screen kiosk in the foyer explains the story behind the lion and also features information on Penn State sports, the history of the Libraries, and quizzes on Penn State, agricultural sciences, and more.

Outside the Pattee entrance, a relief sculpture bears a quotation from famed poet Thomas Carlyle: "The true university is a collection of books." At Penn State, the true library is that and the multitude of other research resources for steadfast and hearty learners.

· · · · ·

A True Pennsylvanian

Fred Waring, known as "the man who taught America how to sing," was a Penn State pioneer. Waring got his start at Penn State as an architectural engineering student, a background that helped him develop the famous "Waring Blendor" and the instant steam iron. More familiar to most are his accomplishments in the recording industry. One of his first auditions was for Thomas Edison in the early 1920s, and his first recording was the theme song, "Sleep," for the Victor Talking Machine Company. Waring was the first to record with a female singer, to feature vocalists with an orchestra, and to combine orchestra and glee club. He performed for sixty-nine years with The Pennsylvanians, with whom he recorded 1,500 songs and one hundred albums.

Waring served his alma mater as a trustee and Distinguished Alumnus. He conducted the world-famous Fred Waring Choral Workshop at Penn State in his later years, and in 1984 he designated Penn State to house his collection of archives and memorabilia. On July 29, 1984, shortly after taping a concert for Penn State's public television station, Fred Waring died.

The Fred Waring Collection, known as "Fred Waring's America," is part of the University Libraries' Special Collections Library and is housed in Pattee. It contains a discography and historical memorabilia—and even a collection of cartoons depicting Waring—that reflect the performer's nearly seventy-year career as a choral conductor and showman. But Waring's is not the only collection at the University Libraries.

Selected Collections and Archives in the Special Collections Library of the University Libraries

100th Pennsylvania Volunteers Civil War Collection
A Few Good Women Oral History Collection
Allison-Shelly Collection (German literature in English translation)
American Sociological Association Archives

Chemical Engineering would not be considered under any circumstance. It later was learned that he had also turned down Fred Waring.

Though funds were scarce, a few fortunate students did obtain WPA jobs doing cleanup work in professors' laboratories. In this fashion one became better acquainted with the professor but also saw what a working lab was like. Our class had a unique opportunity: we built and set up the Chemical Engineering Laboratory in the old Walker Lab (no longer in existence). We learned much more than had we been merely running the experiments.

One of the most notable moments in my four years was in my sophomore Chemical Engineering class. Our text was a hefty volume, and prominently on one of the pages were listed the Three Laws of Chemical Engineering. Imagine the gasp when Professor Fenske began the class one morning with "Take your books and cross out the Second Law." It stated that matter could neither be created nor destroyed— and this had been proved wrong by nuclear science.

A few of my many great memories of Penn State.

—BILL GRIFFIN, CLASS OF '36

WHEN WE WERE freshmen (1998–99), my friend Monica and I liked to really prepare for the PSU football games by getting all dolled up—Penn State colors everywhere, including our faces! We even offered our face-painting services to passersby at the games. Often we would pose for random cameras because our Penn State spirit was literally spelled across our faces. Come senior year, one day when I was at my best friend's apartment, I noticed a photo from one of those freshman games on his counter. I wondered why he had that picture out and where he had gotten it. I looked more closely: Monica and I had been featured in a Penn State parking brochure, three years later! Our PSU spirit remains—four years and many parking brochures later. I still give autographs if anyone needs one!

—KIMBERLY MURPHY, CLASS OF '01

Harry J. Anslinger Papers (narcotics law enforcement)

Samuel Bayard Folk Music Collection

Arnold Bennett Papers

Luther and Jessie Bernard Collection (sociology)

Kenneth Burke Papers

Robert Casey Papers

Eighth Air Force ("The Mighty Eighth") Archive (veterans' collections)

Emblem Book Collection (European volumes, 1531–1700)

Harrington Emerson Papers (efficiency)

Christopher Gaines Memorial Collection (Amish research)

Dale Harris/Florence Goodenough Children's Drawings Collection

Harry B. Henderson Jr. Papers (African American artists)

John Hostetler Papers (Amish/Rural Sociology research)

Charles Jacques Amusement Park Collection

Leon Kneebone Papers (mushroom research)

Arthur O. Lewis Utopia Collection

Fay S. Lincoln architectural photographs

Russell Marker Papers (steroid chemistry research)

John O'Hara Collection and Study

Vance Packard Papers

Penn State University Sports Archives Audio-Visual Collection

Pennsylvania Political Campaign Research Records

Pennsylvania Railroad's Central Division Records, and many subsidiary railroads

Joseph Priestley Collection

Conrad Richter Papers

William Scranton Papers

Ammon Stapleton Collection (Pennsylvania German books)

State College Community Organizations Collection

United Mineworkers of America (UMWA) Archives

United Steelworkers of America (USWA) Records

Jonathan W. White Jr. Papers (honey research)

20 FRANK AND SYLVIA PASQUERILLA SPIRITUAL CENTER (2003) / HELEN EAKIN EISENHOWER CHAPEL (1956; ADDITION 1976)

One of the more striking additions to campus in recent years, the Frank and Sylvia Pasquerilla Spiritual Center was dedicated in 2003. The most notable feature is its masonry light tower, which signifies light as a common symbol for many of the more than forty registered religious groups on campus. The tower, shown here, is at the center of a courtyard that ties together the new center and the adjacent Helen Eakin Eisenhower Chapel. Providing over 50,000 square feet of worship and program space, the multi-faith complex is one of the largest religious centers on a public university campus in the nation—a reflection of the University's commitment to developing mind, body, and spirit.

The Pasquerilla Center was named in honor of the late Frank and Sylvia Pasquerilla of Johnstown, who donated the lead gift of $5 million for the building's construction. Designed by James Oleg Kruhly and Associates, it features a two-story core worship area that can accommodate 477 people, and three adjoining chambers with an additional 260 seats that can be opened to the main area or closed off as separate rooms. The complex includes several program rooms that can be used for prayer, worship, or other functions; two kitchens, one of which is kosher; administrative offices; and ample gathering space outside worship areas.

The Helen Eakin Eisenhower Chapel, the University's original spiritual center, was built in 1956, during the tenure of Penn State's eleventh president, Milton Eisenhower. It was named in honor of his wife, who had died two years earlier. Mrs. Eisenhower had worked to have the chapel built, and it seemed a particularly appropriate memorial. It has long been a popular location for weddings of Penn State alumni.

The arts at Penn State flourished as never before in the early 1960s. The College of Arts and Architecture was formally established in 1963, and Music Building I, the Pavilion Theatre, and the Arts Building all opened between 1963 and 1965.

The 450-seat Playhouse Theatre, housed within the Arts Building (pictured here), is the School of Theatre's largest performance space. It features an unusually wide proscenium arch stage and a hydraulic orchestra pit that can be raised flush with the stage. In addition to its main auditorium, the Arts Building (designed by Eshbach, Pullinger, and Stevens) includes two small studios, one on the first floor used primarily for dance and movement classes, and another in the basement. This studio, Room 6, is used not only for acting classes and rehearsals but also for performances of small workshop productions and student-written plays. The Arts Building also contains offices for the School of Theatre and the Department of Art History as well as the administrative offices of the College of Arts and Architecture.

Music I (also designed by Eshbach, Pullinger, and Stevens) contains the offices of the School of Music, classrooms, rehearsal space, and a choral music library. It houses the 400-seat Esber Recital Hall, as well, which is equipped with a concert pipe organ and a harpsichord. The hall is named for George Esber, brother of local imported-rug expert W. E. Esber. The late W. E. Esber was a pianist and an avid supporter of the School of Music. His donations over the years allowed the school to purchase a nine-foot Bösendorfer concert grand piano (regarded as one of the preeminent keyboard instruments in the world), to create three scholarships for students of the violin or piano, and to maintain and restore the recital hall.

Like its counterpart, Music II (designed by Ewing, Cole, Cherry, and Brott) contains a number of offices and rehearsal and performance spaces. It houses a library of instrumental ensemble music, percussion studios, and—fittingly for one of the most recent additions to the arts at Penn State—technical labs for creating electronic music.

. . . . .

Where the Boys and Girls Are

There honestly is nothing better than emerging from the Forum Building on a picturesque late summer day, sporting a T-shirt, shorts, and flip-flops and immediately being greeted by a surging rain that would make Noah quiver in his robe.

—Mike Walbert, Daily Collegian, April 29, 2002

No student finishes her or his time at Penn State without taking at least one class in the Forum, Willard, or Thomas building—if not one every semester. They may not be architecturally inspiring, but these three buildings are nonetheless the workhorses of University Park instructional space. Many introductory "monster" classes are held in the Forum Building (top). Built for the innovative use of film, video, and slide projection in teaching, each of the Forum's wedge-shaped, theatre-style classrooms holds about four hundred students, who may lounge outside on the building's steps or in the nearby plaza, as seen here. Willard Building (right) has been known to students for decades as a central place to meet. It houses the Department of African and African American Studies and the Department of Labor Studies and Industrial Relations as well as several other academic programs. Students, faculty, and staff can also buy reasonably priced hardware and software in Willard's Microcomputer Order Center. Joab Thomas Building (bottom), the newest of these three staple buildings, is located at the corner of Shortlidge and Pollock roads. Classrooms at Thomas are equipped with VCRs, televisions, overhead projectors, and access to Penn State's mainframe computer system and network and the Internet. Offices for the Eberly College of Science are also found here.

22 STUCKEMAN FAMILY BUILDING FOR THE SCHOOL OF ARCHITECTURE AND LANDSCAPE ARCHITECTURE (2005)

For years, students in the Architecture and Landscape Architecture departments worked away in relative secrecy, hidden from view in the second and third floors of the Engineering Units. But no longer! In 2005 the School of Architecture and Landscape Architecture (SALA) moved into its new home—the spectacular Stuckeman Family Building.

Named for University alumnus H. Campbell "Cal" Stuckeman of Pittsburgh and his late wife, Eleanor Stuckeman, the new building is the first on campus designed to meet the national criteria for certification as environmentally friendly, "sustainable" architecture, adhering to the Leadership in Energy and Environmental Design (LEED) Green Building Rating System.

The most visually striking feature of the building is the portion wrapped in a copper "skin." Conceived as a ribbon, it connects two floors of studio and work space and a linking mezzanine of review and gallery spaces. The design permits optimum daylight and creates a ghostly nighttime effect from the outside when the windows glow from the designers' all-nighters. The copper skin is also recyclable, should the building be demolished years down the road.

SALA was established in 1997 to encourage cooperation and collaboration between the Departments of Architecture and Landscape Architecture. The Stuckeman Family Building physically integrates the two departments under one roof, reuniting them as well with related departments within the College of Arts and Architecture. Other features of the building include a model building workshop, an exhibition gallery, an amphitheater for lectures and conferences, and an arts and architecture library. A number of public spaces are designed so that teaching and exhibitions can extend outside the building into the surrounding landscape. Altogether, the new building doubles the amount of space previously available to SALA.

23 PALMER MUSEUM OF ART (1972; MAJOR RENOVATION 1993)

Surprisingly, the largest public art museum between Philadelphia and Pittsburgh is Penn State's own Palmer Museum of Art. Designed by Charles W. Moore—a pioneer of postmodern architecture in the United States—in association with Arbonies King Vlock, the Palmer represents a significant expansion and enhancement of the University's first Museum of Art. The old building is still visible behind the new entrance. Though the original museum displayed things aesthetic, it was not a major architectural landmark on

I GREW UP IN a rural town in Pennsylvania and was nervous upon entering Penn State as a first-year student. I initially knew nobody, but was instantly accepted by new friends from New Jersey, Texas, Iowa, Cyprus, and everywhere in between. My fondest PSU memories include the many pranks my friends and I (often the guys versus the girls) played on each other in Beaver Hall and Nittany Apartments.

I especially recall two entertaining moments in which my "friends" were particularly savvy. They put me in a tall trash can and proceeded to leave me in an elevator, then sent me to the top floor of the dorm to greet other students in my awkward state. One of my female pals became the unsuspecting victim of another comical prank in which the guys wrote a fictitious request for housing personnel to change my friend's soiled mattress, unbeknownst to her. When the housing employees appeared at my friend's door, she was shocked and we were all overcome with laughter. Although we sometimes got a bit carried away with our practical jokes, we used these tactics to help us cope with the stresses we faced in college, and this lightheartedness has prepared us to effectively handle the challenges we currently face in our lives. Most important, we formed unique bonds of friendship as Penn Staters. I started my PSU career alone and left with the sweetest, most amazing friends I could ever wish for. We Are . . . Thankful.

—TRACI FRYE, CLASS OF '02

campus. According to Professor Craig Zabel of the Department of Art History, it was "universally decreed uninviting, uninteresting, and ugly. People talked about engulfing, hiding, or destroying it." It was also too small. The design and size of the galleries allowed for the display of only a fraction of the permanent collection.

In 1986, Barbara and James Palmer of State College came to the rescue. Their generous gift initiated a building campaign that culminated in the opening of the new museum in 1993. Renamed the Palmer Museum of Art, it features eleven galleries, a 150-seat auditorium, and a gift shop. The most striking feature of Moore's design is the museum's dramatic entrance. The massive bronze lion's paws that guard the steps of the museum were created by Paul Bowdin, a Pittsburgh sculptor.

Today, the museum's permanent collection includes more than five thousand artworks that span more than thirty-five centuries of paintings, drawings, photographs, sculptures, and other works from the United States, Europe, Asia, Africa, and South America. Asian ceramics, painting, and printmaking are represented, as are ancient objects from Europe, Africa, and the Near East. Museum visitors can contemplate a world of art at the Palmer—from works by the "old masters" of Europe to nineteenth-century American landscapes to modernist and contemporary pieces, Japanese woodblock prints, jade sculptures from China, sculptures and masks from sub-Saharan Africa, and ancient pottery from Peru.

Adjacent to the museum is the Hamer Sculpture Garden (1993), named for State College businessman and arts supporter Donald Hamer. The garden, designed by George Dickie, gracefully showcases sculptures situated among a variety of trees and ornamental grasses.

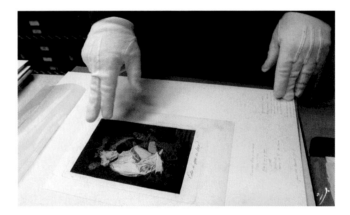

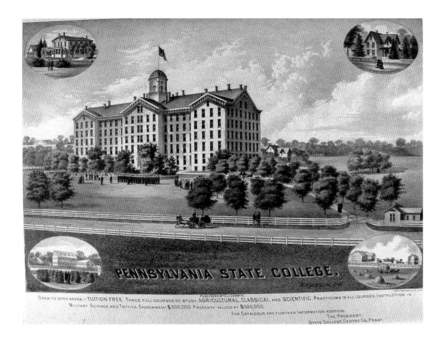

Pennsylvania Print Collection

One of several major collections at the Palmer Museum of Art is the O'Connor/Yeager Collection of Pennsylvania Prints, also known as "The Tavern Collection." The late John C. O'Connor and Ralph M. Yeager, original owners of The Tavern Restaurant in downtown State College, began collecting prints in the 1950s, displaying selections from their collection in the restaurant for many years. The first major exhibition of the collection was held at the museum in 1980.

Through a combination of donation and purchase from the collectors, this collection of 330 prints was added to the museum's permanent collection in 1986. It includes lithographs, engravings, aquatints, photogravures, and woodcuts created by artists of the late eighteenth, nineteenth, and early twentieth centuries. These prints depict Pennsylvania town views, portraits, and historical scenes, offering a unique glimpse into Pennsylvania's past.

The 1878 view pictured here was published by C. J. Corbin and Company. The lithographic work, hand-colored by M. Traubel, was done by the Thomas Hunter Company of Philadelphia. Corbin enlisted well-known artist W. W. Denslow to sketch the views on location. (Denslow was the illustrator for the first edition of the Wizard of Oz.)

As graduation grew closer, however, I began to sense that time was indeed passing and my balcony days were numbered. Funny as it may sound, in those final days before graduation, I cared less for keg parties and riots and more for Old Main sunsets. I'd sit for hours on my balcony, not quite sure what I was hoping to see. Looking back, I realize that I wasn't trying to see anything. Instead, I was taking a mental photograph, trying to create a still frame of not only the perfect Penn State view but also the perfect Penn State moment.

When I return to Happy Valley now, I still stop to see all of the traditional Penn State landmarks—the Lion Shrine, the Creamery, and Beaver Stadium (now with high-tech scoreboards and fancy skyboxes). But the not-so-public attractions top my list of must-sees on the Penn State tour. For me, nothing brings back memories like driving down Beaver Avenue and looking up at my own personal skybox, the balcony at Apt. 402.

—BETH RINGLER, CLASS OF '01

24 THE CREAMERY (FOUNDED 1889; MOVED TO BORLAND LABORATORY IN 1932; RELOCATED TO FOOD SCIENCE BUILDING, RENAMED BERKEY CREAMERY 2006)

Penn State students and alumni may recall standing in line, summer or winter, for a scoop of Peachy Paterno or Death by Chocolate at the Creamery. But this Penn State institution is more than a simple ice cream shop. For instance, researchers at the Creamery examine how dairy products are affected by processing and storage. The Creamery also sponsors short courses and workshops for professionals in the dairy industry, including the famous "Ice Cream Short Course."

Each year the Creamery produces about 225,000 gallons of ice cream, frozen sherbet, and yogurt, and Creamery workers hand-dip about 750,000 ice cream cones. One of the Creamery's more famous patrons has been President Bill Clinton—a self-professed "big Penn State fan"—who stopped by for some Peachy Paterno during the National Governors' Association Summer Meeting in July 2000. (When Clinton came to Penn State to speak at the 1996 commencement exercises, Creamery workers waived the "no mixing flavors" rule for him: he became the first person ever permitted to have scoops of two different ice cream flavors on a cone.)

The first Creamery was built in 1889 as part of Dean Henry Prentiss Armsby's attempts to improve the College's offerings and research in dairying, and dairy courses offered that year were immediately popular—so much so that the College herds could not make enough milk to meet demand. In 1892, Penn State offered the nation's first college-level instruction in ice cream manufacture. The Creamery moved in 1904, and then again in 1932 to its current location in Borland Laboratory. The salesroom, seen in the photo opposite, was added in 1961, where cheese, milk, yogurt, and other dairy products are available (in addition to hand-dipped or packaged ice cream). In 2004, Penn State's Board of Trustees approved plans for a new Food Science Building at University Park, in order to better facilitate the University's long-standing service to the needs of Pennsylvania's food processing and manu-facturing industries. Designed by IKM Incorporated, and rendered below, the Food Science building houses the new Berkey Creamery, located near the cor-ner of Curtin and Bigler roads. The Berkey Creamery, named in recognition of the generosity of Jeanne (Class of '48) and Earl (PSU Creamery Short Course) Berkey, contains laboratories, classrooms, offices, and pilot-scale processing facilities. Covered outdoor seating and tables, benches, and seatwalls com-plement the new salesroom and café.

MY FATHER GRADUATED from Penn State in 1923. In the mid-1930s, he returned there for a number of summers to pursue a master's degree. My brother, sister, and I were always delighted with the trip from Windber to Penn State because that meant a cone at the Creamery and a romp in Hort Woods before depositing Dad in his room. We reversed the process when we picked him up at the end of the summer. When it came time for me to think of college, no other than Penn State ever entered my mind.

I enrolled in the fall of 1944. Because of the many Army trainees and the Navy's V-12 cadets, I was one of many coeds who ended up in town housing. I lived at Cody Manor on South Allen Street. It was a good starting place for a small-town girl. From there, our house coeds were sent to Jordan Hall for sophomore year.

After joining Gamma Phi Beta sorority, I moved to the Women's Building sorority suite for my last two years. What a wonderful place to live! We were in the midst of the campus, just steps from meals at Mac Hall, events at Schwab Auditorium, and most of our classes. We had our own living room (where four on the floor was the rule), large rooms, a tiny kitchenette, and a kind and understanding housemother. There was a giant ginkgo tree in the front yard that offered shade and a place to lounge in suitable weather. I was saddened to see both tree and house disappear.

My four years at Penn State were the four best years of my life.

—SUZANNE R. ROMIG, CLASS OF '44

Penn State Firsts, 1900–1950

1903   Schwab Auditorium was built—the first structure on campus funded with private money.

1905   Calvin H. Waller, believed to be Penn State's first African American graduate, received a B.A. in agriculture. Official records of racial identities were not kept at that time.

1907   Druids, the first men's honorary "hat" society, was formed.

1910   Froth, a student humor magazine, is published for the first time.

1915   Health service began with the first regular physician and infirmary.

1919   The first coed theatre group on campus, the Penn State Players, was organized. It became the nucleus of the dramatics curriculum.

1922   The Graduate School was established, with Frank D. Kern as its first dean.

1923   W. G. Chambers became the first dean of the newly instituted School of Education.

1926   Chi Omega was chartered as the first national women's fraternity on campus.

1931   The School of Physical Education and Athletics was established; Hugo Bezdek became its first dean.

1934   The first Undergraduate Centers—the beginning of the Commonwealth Campus system—opened in Pottsville and Hazleton.

1938   Carl W. Hasek became the first director of the new Bureau of Business Research.

1947   Extension Services began a program in labor education. Anthony Luchek served as first director.

25 PAVILION THEATRE (1960; ORIGINAL STRUCTURE 1914)

On days when the sun is too strong or the rain too heavy, Creamery customers often scurry across Curtin Road to eat their ice cream on the portico of the Pavilion Theatre. As a performance venue, the Pavilion has operated since the early 1960s, but the structure itself dates back to 1914, when it was erected as Penn State's first Livestock Judging Pavilion. With its much-needed exhibition arena, the Pavilion was the place where students could show farm animals and compete in expos, like the cattle judging shown opposite. Even today, the floor retains a slight convex curve originally intended to channel liquids into gutters around the perimeter of the stage.

The Pavilion is a unique performance space on campus—the brainchild of the late Kelly Yeaton, a former Penn State professor of theatre, who con-

vinced Penn State administrators to transform the building into an arena theatre. Where other auditoriums like Schwab or the Playhouse feature a proscenium arch design (with all of the seats facing the same direction toward the stage), the Pavilion's theatre-in-the-round arrangement offers playgoers a more intimate viewing experience. Seating surrounds the stage on all four sides, meaning that the action of the play literally takes place in the middle of the audience. There is also no buffer between the stage and the seating: when an actor walks to the edge of the stage, she is standing only about a foot away from the front row of the audience. The seating on the western side of the theatre is removable, and, depending on a

play's design, sometimes this space is used to hold part of the set.

In the summer, the Pavilion—along with the Playhouse and the Citizens Bank Theatre—is used by Pennsylvania Centre Stage, a group that gives students a chance to work with theatre professionals from around the country. During the school year, those same three venues are home to the School of Theatre's productions and directing projects. Shows have included everything from Shakespearean tragedy (*Macbeth*) to recent cult hits (*The House of Yes*), from powerful political commentary (*The Crucible*) to undergraduate honors theses (*Answering Machine*). When not in use for performances, the Pavilion and its basement rehearsal studio, where the old meat-cutting laboratories were located, are used for acting and dance classes.

Drama Queens—and Kings

Recognized as a hallmark of Penn State life, the Penn State Thespians was founded in 1897 by Fred Lewis Pattee and John H. Leete—professors of American literature and mathematics—as a men's dramatics club. With few women on campus, and theatrical acting considered unladylike, the group's shows were performed exclusively by men until World War I. Women were included for the first time in the 1918 production of It Pays to Advertise, when there were not enough men available to fill the parts—though one might have wished for women to have been cast in the production pictured here! It was not until 1926 that women would again act on the Thespian stage.

The Penn State Thespians advertises itself as the oldest student organization on campus, though members of La Vie disagree. And if you ask members of Greek organizations, both are incorrect, since fraternities appeared on campus as early as the 1870s, though they were not officially recognized by Penn State's administration until much later. Which is the oldest student organization at Penn State? You decide. . . .

· · · · ·

Vive La Vie!

The first edition of La Vie, the Penn State yearbook, appeared in 1889, a publication of the junior class of 1890. (It did not become a senior class project until 1930.) But wait—doesn't that make La Vie the oldest student organization on campus, not the Penn State Thespians? Since the 1940s, when publication of La Vie was temporarily suspended due to a World War II paper shortage, there has been a good-natured dispute among Thespians and La Vie-ers over which group is the oldest on campus. The Penn State Thespians is the oldest continually active student organization at University Park, but La Vie was founded first.

Armsby Building (1905) | Patterson Building (1903; renovated 1964) | Weaver Building (1915) | Arts Cottage (1889)

Armsby, Patterson, and Weaver buildings are situated on Ag Hill, the site of a number of agricultural buildings and plots northeast of Old Main that is now on the National Register of Historic Places. In the College's early days, barns, the Agricultural Experiment Station, and experimental farms sat on the hill, and Edward Hazlehurst's new buildings—grand brick structures adorned with arches, columns, or turreted roofs—were remarkable additions. Armsby Building, shown here, served as the main agriculture building and was named in 1956 for Henry Prentiss Armsby, the first dean of agriculture (1895–1902). The adjacent Calorimeter Building, holding America's first calorimeter, was designed by Armsby and completed in 1902.

Patterson Building originally held the College's creamery. In 1937, it was named for William Calvin Patterson, Penn State's superintendent of farms (1872–1909). Renovated in 1964, it now contains the main offices and studio/gallery space for faculty, staff, and students in the School of Visual Arts. Weaver Building was named in 1954 for agricultural economist Frederick Pattison Weaver and provided space for the Horticulture Department. It now houses the Department of History and Religious Studies, the Department of Classics and Ancient Mediterranean Studies, and the Department of Latin American Studies as well as the Jewish Studies Program and other academic offices.

The Arts Cottage began life around 1889 as the Agricultural Experiment Station. Designed by Frederick Olds, the building was constructed with funds released by the Hatch Act. It was renovated around 1941 and transformed into the Agricultural Education Building, which later became the Arts Education/Crafts Building. Today, it is known as the Arts Cottage, home of the Art Education program.

Turn Your Head and Moo

Penn State's calorimeter is housed in a small, heavily insulated brick building on Ag Hill. Completed in 1902 under the direction of Dean Henry Armsby, it was used in the development and improvement of livestock feed. The first agricultural instrument of its kind, the calorimeter operated on a simple principle: "What goes in must come out." Measuring "what came out" against the food, water, and air that an animal consumed allowed the net energy or production value of feed to be determined. Decades later, the calorimeter was used to study protein in the human diet.

27 LIFE SCIENCES BUILDING (2004) / CHEMISTRY BUILDING (2004)

The idea behind the Life Sciences Building emerged nearly a decade before its actual construction. In 1995, the University officially established a Life Sciences Consortium. The group brought together more than five hundred scientists from seven different colleges: Health and Human Development, Science, Medicine, Agricultural Sciences, Engineering, Liberal Arts, and Earth and Mineral Sciences. Its goal was to "move forward boldly in the life sciences by supporting the best and most innovative ideas and people, regardless of their academic home and discipline."

The program has been a success, yielding research developments in areas like neuroscience and immunology. But by its very cross-college nature, the consortium has suffered from a lack of centralized resources and information. The solution to this problem came in the form of a new Life Sciences Building (designed by Bower Lewis Thrower Architects/Payette). Ground was broken for Life Sciences on October 5, 2001, near the intersection of Shortlidge and Pollock roads. Its facilities include classrooms, a 182-seat auditorium, and thirty-eight laboratories as well as office space and conference rooms. Across the street from the Life Sciences Building sits the new Chemistry Building, with a glassed-in aerial walkway—the Verne M. Willaman Gateway to the Sciences—connecting the two and fostering further collaboration.

As part of a trend discouraging vehicular traffic on campus, a portion of Shortlidge Road, which once ran directly through the campus from College Avenue to Park Avenue, has been converted to a brick-paved pedestrian walkway and plaza. The plaza visually connects the new buildings to the nearby Thomas and Ritenour buildings, and it features a number of plantings as well as the Penn State seal and a large clock—the gift of the Class of 1952.

28 COTTAGES

Spruce Cottage (1890) | Pine Cottage (c. 1888) | Ihlseng Cottage (c. 1898)

In the mid-nineteenth century, Centre County was chosen as the site for the Farmers' High School partly because of its remote, rural character. But as enrollment increased and the school grew into The Pennsylvania State College, housing shortages became a problem. Like their students, a growing number of faculty members found their easiest—and often only—living options to be on campus. Spruce, Pine, and Ihlseng Cottages were some of those options. Sharp contrasts to much of the campus's grand architecture, the three quaint cottages remain to this day.

From its construction in 1890 until its relocation in 1937–38, Spruce Cottage stood on the site of what is now Osmond Laboratory. Designed by Frederick Olds, the cottage's first occupants were George Pond, the dean of

what would become the College of Chemistry and Physics, and his family. (Pond's wife ran a school from the cottage for "youngsters judged too small or too young to make the hike to the public school on South Fraser Street.") After Pond's death in 1920, the cottage was called Guest House; trustees and other important visitors to the campus lodged there until the opening of the Nittany Lion Inn in 1931. It has been used for a number of other purposes since then. Renamed Spruce Cottage in 1949, it now hosts the McNair Scholars Program and the Talent Search Program.

Pine Cottage was built around 1888 for the school's military commander, Lieutenant Paggue. In 1917, it became home to Robert Sackett, dean of the School of Engineering, until he retired in 1937. Like Spruce Cottage, Pine was moved around 1937–38 to make way for Osmond Lab. The building now houses offices for the Pennsylvania Commission on Sentencing.

Ihlseng Cottage, pictured on page 91, was built in 1898 as a residence for Magnus Ihlseng, the first dean of the School of Mines. Ihlseng paid for the cottage's construction himself; when he resigned in 1900, he sold the cottage to the College. Other deans of mines lived in the cottage until 1914, when it was converted to an infirmary. (A scarlet fever outbreak in 1913 had convinced the College that such a hospital was necessary for the students, and the College Health Service opened in 1915.) The infirmary had a waiting room, operating room, and dispensary on the first floor; up to six bed patients could be cared for on the second floor. Students could receive medical attention at the cottage, but only during limited hours. Such care was free, although medical "house calls" to students' rooms were $.50 for a daytime visit and $1.00 for a nighttime visit. Bed patients at the infirmary paid $1.25 per day, with the money from these fees placed in the "maintenance fund" of the Health Service. After the infirmary's operations were moved elsewhere on campus in 1929—including to the College's new hospital, now known as Ritenour Building—Ihlseng Cottage held a variety of departments in the liberal arts. Since 1971, it has been the home of the Institute for Arts and Humanities.

Little Cottage on the Campus

"First Cottage," also known as "The Little Yellow House" (pictured opposite), was the first cottage constructed on campus. Built in 1856 by a campus carpenter, it was located in the vicinity of Burrowes Building. It originally housed the carpenter, then farm help, and then faculty. The second story was added in 1880. Frances Atherton—wife of University president George Atherton—lived there after her husband's death in 1906. Later, the cottage was moved off campus to Adams Street in College Heights.

29 EBERLY COLLEGE OF SCIENCE

Davey Laboratory (1969) | Althouse Laboratory (1970) | Mueller Laboratory (1963) | Pond Laboratory (1917) | McAllister Building (1904) | Frear Building (1938; renovated 1968, 1972) | Osmond Laboratory (1938; renovated 1973) | Whitmore Laboratory (1951) | Chandlee Laboratory (1964, renovated 1970) | Buckhout Laboratory (1929, renovated 1952, 1970) | Wartik Laboratory (1987)

Penn State's Eberly College of Science comprises the Departments of Astronomy and Astrophysics, Biology, Biochemistry and Molecular Biology, Chemistry, Mathematics, Physics, and Statistics. It has produced world-class research for 145 years—nearly since Penn State's inception. Members of the College's faculty were the first to "see" the atom, discover a practical method

to synthesize the hormone progesterone, and find planets outside our solar system. College researchers designed the Hobby-Eberly telescope, one of the largest optical telescopes in the world. And a new NASA satellite, the Swift Gamma Ray Burst Explorer launched in late 2004, is yet another Penn State collaboration. Researchers at Penn State built and tested the Swift's X-ray and UV/optical telescopes, and the satellite is operated by the Penn State team from a mission operations center located on the campus.

Near the HUB stand the core buildings that serve the College's seven academic departments—and that provide evidence of a historic boom in higher education during the 1960s and 1970s. Mueller, for instance, was erected in 1963, Davey in 1969, and Althouse in 1970. But several of the science buildings date back to the pre-war era. Pond, built in 1917 and renovated several times since, was named for George Gilbert Pond, dean of the School of Natural Science and a professor in chemistry (1888–1920). McAllister is more than one hundred years old. It was built in 1904 and named after Hugh McAllister, one of Penn State's founders and a charter member of the Board of Trustees (1855–73). Frear was built in 1938 and remodeled in 1968 and 1972; it took the name of William Frear, a professor of agricultural chemistry who also ran the Agricultural Experiment Station.

As imposing as these buildings are, they attest to lively research and outreach efforts by students and faculty alike. On the ground floor of Osmond, curious visitors will find hands-on exhibits demonstrating "virtual images" (via concave paraboloidal mirrors), chaos theory, and electrodynamics, as well as halls filled with portraits of Nobel Prize winners. A glassed-in cubicle in Whitmore has open office hours for students and is decorated with Polaroids of the winners of the "clever chemist award" in general chemistry. Posters of research projects demonstrate students' interest in analyzing everything from mouthwash and sports drinks to the output of fuel cells and the ion effect. And the roof of Davey, shown on page 93, is open to stargazers on clear Friday nights.

How's That for Distance Education?

On May 3, 1998, the space shuttle Columbia landed at Kennedy Space Center in Florida, safely returning James A. Pawelczyk to earth after completing 256 orbits of the planet. Pawelczyk, associate professor of physiology and kinesiology in the College of Health and Human Development, was the first Penn State faculty member to go into space. During the mission, which was devoted to studies of the brain, nervous system, and behavior, Pawelczyk conducted experiments with rats and mice, but he also was spun in a rotating chair at forty-five miles per hour to explore how the balance organs in the inner ear adapt to space flight. He had his sleep cycle, nighttime movement, breathing patterns, blood pressure, and heart rate recorded to help determine if altered breathing patterns contribute to the difficulties astronauts have sleeping in weightlessness.

Pawelczyk is one shining example of a growing portfolio of NASA–Penn State projects. In 1989, Penn State was the lead institution in establishing the Pennsylvania Space Grant Consortium, a component of NASA's National Space Grant College and Fellowship Program. Since 2002 Penn State has ranked among the top ten universities in the nation in terms of NASA-funded research, with annual research expenditures in excess of $20 million. The research being done at Penn State spans a broad range of programs within the Colleges of Earth and Mineral Sciences, Engineering, Science, and Health and Human Development as well as the Applied Research Laboratory. Strong research programs are presently ongoing in astrobiology, propulsion, climate evolution, rotorcraft technologies, human effects of space flight, novel materials and processing for space applications, and astronomy and astrophysics.

Another feather in Penn State's space cap came in 2004 with the launching of the Swift Gamma Ray Burst Explorer. Scientists in the Eberly College of Science built two scientific instruments for the Swift—which tracks the most powerful explosions in the universe—and Penn State is hosting the Swift mission operations center.

3O HUB–ROBESON CENTER

Hetzel Union Building (HUB) (1955; major renovations 1973, 1983, 1999) | Paul Robeson Cultural Center (founded 1972; renovated 1986; joined to HUB 1999)

Perhaps the most conspicuous and well-known building on campus aside from Old Main, the Hetzel Union Building has evolved many times over the years. Its present incarnation has existed only since 1999, but the lineage of the HUB dates all the way back to 1920, when the Penn State Student Union was founded to ensure space for student organizations and events. For two decades, the group grew in both strength and numbers. The "new" Old Main, built in 1929–30, contained offices and meeting space for student groups as well as a student lounge. But over time, administrative offices pushed the students out—and no space had been allocated in Old Main for dances or similar events.

In the mid-1940s, following World War II, Penn State brought the Temporary Union Building—the TUB—onto campus as a student activity center. (The TUB had been, in fact, a USO recreation building in Lebanon, Pennsylvania, before Penn State bought it and had it dismantled, shipped to campus, and reassembled—but that's another story!) It featured not only a snack area and lounges but also a stage and a dance floor. In the meanwhile, after several unsuccessful attempts in the 1940s to finance a permanent student union building via special levies on undergraduates, in 1950, the All-College Cabinet finally managed to persuade students to vote in favor of a plan that would bill each student ten dollars every semester until sufficient funds to build a union had been raised. After delays caused by the Korean War, construction on the union building finally began in 1953. The HUB officially opened on March 15, 1955. (Its name honors Ralph Dorn Hetzel, president of Penn State between 1927 and 1947.) With amenities similar to the HUB of today, the union building of the 1950s featured a ballroom, a television area, a music listening area, a bank of pay phones, a cafeteria, and the offices of many student organizations.

The HUB has been through several renovations, but the largest and most recent of these was the addition of 91,000 square feet of space (including a terrace for outdoor dining, shown here). The centerpiece of this addition was the Paul Robeson Cultural Center, which, with its motto "Respect and Responsibility," is committed to promoting educational excellence and cultural diversity.

The Robeson Center grew out of the student-run Black Cultural Center and was intended to offer support to black Penn State students and promote understanding across a racial divide. The Black Cultural Center was officially established on campus in 1972 and was headquartered in the Walnut Building (the new name of the TUB). The center changed its name in 1975 to honor Paul Robeson (see below) and to signify a broader mission, one that would foster awareness of the diversity of cultures on campus and help all minority students, regardless of their ethnic background, acclimate to life at the University. In 1986, the building was renovated, and it, too, took a new name: the Paul Robeson Cultural Center. And in 1999, it underwent enormous expansion as it joined with the HUB. The facility now includes Heritage Hall, the Robeson Gallery, a library, and and office space for a number of student associations. It offers diverse public programming, including films, concerts, and art exhibitions.

With its galleries, food courts, spacious and comfortable study areas, game room, pool hall, and TV lounge, the HUB–Robeson Center is a veritable mecca of student life. Despite its physical changes over the years, the HUB remains what it has always been: a place for all students to meet, eat, study, and (on especially long days) sleep.

· · · · ·

Emperor Robeson

As an athlete, lawyer, actor, singer, and political activist, Paul Leroy Bustill Robeson (1898–1976) was the most widely recognized African American of the 1930s and 1940s. Robeson is perhaps most commonly remembered for his deep baritone voice singing "Ol' Man River" in the musical Show Boat—*as well as for his award-winning roles in both the Broadway and film versions of Eugene O'Neill's* Emperor Jones *and in* Othello, *the longest-running Shakespeare play in Broadway history. A friend of U.S. president Harry Truman and an enemy of Senator Joe McCarthy, Robeson was a national symbol and a cultural leader in the wars against fascism and racism. While he never attended Penn State, Robeson performed here many times. In this 1940 photo, he poses for a local sculptor.*

Going Good into That Gentle Thursday

What began as a speech communications project and a series of spontaneous jam sessions to protect the Vietnam War evolved into a Penn State phenomenon that lasted for a decade. In the third week of every April from 1970 to 1980, thousands of students gathered on the Old Main and HUB lawns to celebrate Gentle Thursday. The event was a sort of miniature Woodstock, promoting community and peace and eventually hosting myriad musical acts, one of which is pictured here. Like other contemporaneous festivals, Gentle Thursday, too, saw its share of substance-fueled revelry. Authorities tolerated the ubiquitous alcohol and hallucinogens in the early years, but as the 1970s moved to a close, the event became less about peace and goodwill toward the planet and more about the party. Concerns over drug abuse led to the cancellation of Gentle Thursday in 1981, and despite several attempts in the early 1980s to revive the festival, organizers never found a way to counter the changing sociopolitical climate. Movin' On, a daylong event held on the HUB lawn every spring since the late 1980s, is in some ways the successor to Gentle Thursday. The concert features a long bill of musicians, ranging from obscure local bands to internationally known groups. But long gone are the components of political and social activism of Gentle Thursday, not to mention the sense of peace, freedom, and spontaneity so cherished in the early 1970s.

·　·　·　·　·

On Top of Old Coaly

The skeleton of Old Coaly, the legendary mule who hauled limestone from Old Quarry to build the original Old Main, currently resides on the first floor of the HUB–Robeson Center. A loyal and hardworking Penn Stater from 1857 until his death on New Year's Day, 1893, Coaly was so popular with students that they recognized him as their informal mascot—long before the Nittany Lion roared onto the scene—and his remains were preserved.

The remains of Old Quarry can also be seen as a depression in the earth on the southeast corner of the Old Main lawn. The area, later landscaped as a natural bowl, was used as an open-air theatre for pageants, plays, and college ceremonies.

Ritenour Building (1929; addition 1956) / Grange Building (1930; renovated 1966, 1973) / Boucke Building (1955)

The 1920s saw an unprecedented explosion in enrollment at Penn State. Students and staff were swiftly outgrowing the already limited resources for housing and services, and the administration struggled to keep up. After President Sparks's departure, Penn State's Board of Trustees chose John Martin Thomas to serve as the College's president—in the hope that he, as an experienced fund-raiser, would oversee a significant expansion of the school's buildings and facilities. And indeed, Thomas oversaw Penn State's first private fund-raising campaign: an emergency building fund drive. By 1928, planning had begun for improvements to the clinic and dispensary located in the student union building, and in 1929, work began on Ritenour Building (pictured here), designed by Charles Klauder.

Around the same time, Klauder's Grange Memorial Dormitory for Girls—now simply called Grange Building—was also under construction. Statistics from 1922 showed that for every one woman accepted to Penn State, two equally qualified applicants were turned away due to lack of housing. The one women's dorm and the five cottages that had been converted to women's housing (i.e., sorority houses) were filled beyond capacity, though the number of women applying continued to increase. The College sought funding for the new dormitory from the Pennsylvania State Grange, an organization formed in the nineteenth century to assist farmers and to improve the lives of rural families. Recognizing Penn State's many contributions to the field of agriculture, the Grange agreed to assist the College. The Grange Building is no longer a dormitory, but it continues to play an important part in undergraduate life, housing the Multicultural Resource Center, the Division of

Undergraduate Studies, the Center for Arts and Crafts, and the production offices of *La Vie*.

Boucke Building, built in 1955 and designed by N. Grant Nicklas Jr., not only serves as a general-purpose classroom building but also contains an impressive number of offices and services, including the University Fellowships Office; the Center for Adult Learner Services; the University Learning Center (containing the Math Center and the Writing Center); two computer labs; the Center for Women Students; the Lesbian, Gay, Bisexual, Transgender and Ally Student Resource Center; Residence Life; and assistance programs for intensive English communication. It originally housed the College of Business Administration and is named for economist Oswald Boucke.

· · · · ·

"The Best Room at Penn State": Grange Building

"I caught nine mice and picked up many more splinters on my feet from the rough floor in McAllister Hall," wrote Margaret Griffin Aschman in 1931. But she wasn't complaining. At the rate women were enrolling in The Pennsylvania State College, finding dormitory rooms for them all had become a major challenge.

During the 1920s, women were entering the College at a brisk pace. McAllister Hall had already been converted into a women's dorm in 1915, but another was urgently needed, and the College did not have the necessary funding to undertake such a project. Fortunately, the Pennsylvania Grange, part of the national organization dedicated to improving the lot of farmers and enriching the lives of the rural population, took on the task. The Grange's purpose in raising the money was to show its appreciation for the agricultural services that the College provided—and to demonstrate that its members "think more of their boys and girls than they do of their horses and cattle."

Through the sale of 42,000 newly created Pennsylvania State Grange cookbooks, as well as membership gifts, the Grange announced that it had raised $100,000 to contribute to a new women's dormitory. It would be heralded as the most outstanding fund-raising achievement of any state Grange of its time.

On June 15, 1928, ground was broken on a field that was being used by Pennsylvania farmers as a vegetable gardening experiment. The architect for the new building was Charles Klauder, who had designed a number of other Penn State landmark buildings. A year later, 102 women moved into Grange Memorial Dormitory. Compared to the two other women's dorms on campus, Women's Building and McAllister Hall, it was luxurious indeed. Each floor had a kitchenette, where dormmates would prepare supper. To Elizabeth Walter Otis, who lived there from 1933 to 1934, it was her "good fortune" to live in the new hall.

> After my freshman year on the fourth floor of Mac Hall, [Grange] seemed very elegant. The mahogany furniture was most impressive. The double desk was spacious and more conducive to studying—certainly an improvement over the small desks we had used in Mac Hall. The lobby was beautifully furnished and an attractive spot to entertain a guest or for your guest to wait until you appeared.

And like many residents before her, Elizabeth Bergstein, who lived in Grange from 1946 to 1948, believed that she had the best dorm room at Penn State.

> We had the top floor room on the far left. . . . Surely there could not have been a better room on campus. It was large with a partial wall across the middle; it divided the two twin beds from an area toward the door that had two desks that faced each other. There were two other rooms on the top. And one nice big bathroom. We had it "made."

During the 1950s, Grange residents, like most young women everywhere, found ways to get around restrictive rules for activities of highest priority. Daisy Reiter, who lived in the dorm from 1954 to 1957, recalls that time.

> Facing the outside front of the building on the third floor was a small roof ledge where the sun shone most of the afternoon. We would sunbathe there. Thank heavens we were never discovered or reported. We were not allowed in public in shorts, let alone to sunbathe in public.

That would be the last decade that Grange would be used exclusively for women. When several more women's residence halls were built during the postwar boom, Grange Hall was converted into graduate housing and then eventually to office space. But for many women, including Ms. Reiter, living in Grange Memorial Dormitory was a treasured

HOW CAN I EVER FORGET my unceremonious arrival in State College as an eighteen-year-old Connecticut Yankee fifty-five years ago? First of all, I was still working at my summer job when I received notice from a professor of naval science, asking why the heck I hadn't arrived yet (or words to that effect). Until that time I had had no idea when classes were supposed to start.

I left work that same day, packed a trunk and a suitcase, and took the train from Bridgeport, Connecticut, to Lewistown. Then I hopped on the mountain jitney that careened through Seven Mountains and left me standing on the sidewalk at the Corner Room.

Next question: "Where is Dorm 44?" Never have I felt so alone and "shapeless in the hands of fate." Fortunately, two upperclassmen realized my dilemma and carried my trunk—and I the suitcase—about a mile through campus to the dorm. I forget what happened the next several days, but I had found my home way out on the frontier in Happy Valley.

I had had my choice of six colleges, choosing Penn State College because of Navy ROTC, Chemical Engineering, a big student body (7,000), big-time football (versus Lafayette or Bucknell), and girls (not necessarily in that order). Little did I know that at the time there were five guys for every girl!

But things worked out.

—ARNOLD C. GASCHE, CLASS OF '52

time and created memories such as this one from the 1950s: "When boys and girls became pinned (engaged), it was customary for the fraternity to present the girl with a dozen roses and a candlelight serenade. I remember the fraternity brothers standing on the large porch in the back, singing to an open window."

32 SCHREYER HONORS COLLEGE, ATHERTON HALL (1938; EXPANSION 2000)

Atherton Hall was built to be the fourth women's dormitory and named for President Atherton's wife, Frances Washburne Atherton, in recognition of her kindness in reaching out to women students. In later years, it served as a residence for single graduate students before being turned over to the University Scholars Program.

The seeds of an honors college were planted in the mid-1970s, but it was not until an unprecedented grant of $30 million from William A. and Joan L. Schreyer in 1997 that the Schreyer Honors College became a reality. Originally conceived as a pre-college enrichment program in 1975, the program was reinvented in 1979 to become a faculty-based "advising-intensive program" that would be open to all Penn State students, regardless of major or campus. The program, then called the University Scholars Program (USP), was spearheaded by Professor Paul Axt of the Department of Mathematics. It encouraged high-scoring students to enroll at the University and featured additional classes and academic work, honors supplements, a senior thesis requirement, and multiple windows of opportunity to enter the program.

In the early 1980s, the USP attracted hundreds of students—and by the mid-1980s, the University counted approximately 1,400 Scholars. Recognizing the growth of the USP and its need for a residential community, in 1984 the University established Atherton Hall as Scholars Housing. In 1996, Penn State President Graham Spanier proposed to increase the program's size dramatically—and the following year saw the founding of the Schreyer Honors College. Today, more honors courses are offered than ever before, and the College's enrollment has an upper limit of 1,800 students.

The recently renovated and expanded site now houses the Schreyer Honors College's offices as well as students. A long staircase from College Avenue leads up to the building, with outdoor benches offering quiet places for reading or conversation. The College's Grandfather Clock Lounge (or GCL) is a favorite spot for lectures, receptions, and musical events as well as the weekly staff meetings for *Problem Child*, a student literary magazine.

IN AUTUMN 1963, when freshmen still wore beanies, it was the tradition for upperclassmen to stop a frosh on the sidewalk and ask questions about the location of campus buildings and landmarks. A trick question often posed was "Where is Galen Hall?" Well, there was no Galen Hall. This question would stump and frustrate nervous freshmen. The "correct" response should have been "In Rec Hall," for Galen Hall was *not* a building but rather the star quarterback on the football team. And we all knew, or should have known, that in 1963 football players hung out in Rec Hall. Ironically, Galen Hall returned to University Park in 2004 as the new offensive coordinator of the Nittany Lions. If freshmen still wore beanies, wouldn't it be fun to pose this familiar question once again: "Where is Galen Hall?"

—SYLVESTER KOHUT JR.,
CLASS OF '64

WHAT ENDURES
THE LANDSCAPE AT UNIVERSITY PARK

GABRIEL WELSCH

Imagine what William Waring must have seen, looking north from College Avenue in 1855—the hill ascending in a tumult of remnant fencerows, huge boulders, and the stumps of trees burned for charcoal to fuel Centre Furnace. For the four years he served as Penn State's first "landscape architect," he would struggle with inconsistent budgets, the presence of quarry pits scarring the hill, a dearth of funds for the purchase of even basic shade trees, and the harsh terrestrial realities of a most difficult plot on which to work.

To what extent could he anticipate campus as it looks and feels today? Did he foresee how you might remember crossing the southern sidewalk in front of Old Main lawn? Now, if it is early enough in the day, you hear only branches knocking lightly, far ahead, or the hush of leaves against one another. You might smell viburnums if it is May, or you might be stunned by the new green of the lawn in April. In winter, you might see each limb of elm and oak articulated with snow, or spruce needles rimed in November frost. If the day is clear, the elm branch tips will etch the sky into a window of blue glass. If it is autumn, then you walk amidst gold—showers of toothed leaves, their veins bronze with age. Regardless of the season, if you look across the lawn at Old Main, you are hit with the abundance of sky, the air moving between you and the building, the serenity of space and nature and vision brought together to ensure that you remember, for the rest of your life, what it feels like to walk on that lawn.

That feeling is no accident. For the last century and a half, virtually every person who has managed aspects of Penn State's landscape has agreed on a few things. First, that the campus should be leafy and, once the grounds were sufficiently renowned for their leafiness, that such a trademark was worth preserving and funding. Second, that subsequent plantings would complement both variety and look among the populations of plants on campus. While flowers would not take their place in the landscape until the Oswald administration (1970–82) and would not fully emerge as a central feature of the landscape until the 1990s, when they did arrive they, too, were integrated with the overall plan.

The plan started with William Waring. The son of an apothecary in his native England, Waring came to the United States in the 1830s, probably carrying with him a certain cutting of a willow tree taken from the poet Alexander Pope's garden. He arrived knowing several languages (among them Latin, Greek, and German), how to play the flute, and the newest methods of farming, and he was dedicated to spreading knowledge. In the two decades before his involvement with the beginnings of the Farmers' High School, Penn State's original name, he taught in surrounding towns, including Bellefonte and Boalsburg, and he established a farm in Oak Hall near Cedar Run. Somewhere along the way, presumably, he developed an ethic that would lead him to concern regarding the environment in which students studied. William Waring wrote the first book published in Centre County, *The Fruit Grower's Handbook* (1851).

Waring's goals went beyond ambience, though that was a concern. He desired that the campus should be a practical environment, providing examples of good land-use practices and a number of plants as examples for study. While he did not, like later planners, think the campus should be an arboretum (for it was at this stage but one building and a lot of semi-cleared land), he held the conviction that plantings be practical.

The plants most often credited to Waring are Old Willow—a descendant of the Pope willow, its original location marked by a plaque on the Mall near Old Main—and the American elms. He also left one other trademark planting. Waring thought hedges were important for the habitats of birds; he was one of many concerned about the dwindling numbers of birds in Centre County due to the number of Pennsylvania's trees falling to fuel furnaces.

A snowy Mall

Hedges cordoned off sections of lawns and helped guide pedestrian traffic as well. Therefore, hedges around Old Main and at the end of the Pugh Street mall (what used to be known as McAllister Walk), near College Avenue, may not have among their constituent plants the original clumps of barberry, but they do possess the palimpsest of original intent. Waring's preferred shrub plant was the barberry, perhaps because it was thick with brambles and unlikely to be traversed, but more likely because of what it offered birds.

The American elms currently along the Pugh Street mall are not original to their site either, but they have been replaced several times because of how important that particular shade allée became to alumni, students seeking shade, the local postcard market, and the people who recruit new students. The planting of elms was perhaps institutionalized because of the ideas of Charles N. Lowrie, a landscape architect and author of the University's first campus and landscape development plan.

In 1907, Lowrie wrote *A Report and Plan for the Campus and Grounds of the Pennsylvania State College*, and in it he admired the "stately elms" of Harvard Yard and the echoes of Jefferson at the University of Virginia, characterizing both places as having benefited from a cohesive vision and subsequent development that remained true to the vision. The Pennsylvania State College had, by that time, been operating with a vision shared yet not articulated as such. President Fraser had tried to contract the famous American progenitor of landscape architecture, Frederick Law Olmstead, but could not afford him. The next president, James Calder, established "Calder's walk"—a line of oaks running along what is now Pollock Road—and a few other professors planted some tree groupings, but there was little else. Waring's hedges, elms, and Old Willow remained, alongside the lawn in front of Old Main that had taken the place of corn and potato fields—but there was little else to bring cohesion to the look of the campus.

Lowrie wrote of a plan for a campus that would be "presenting at all stages of growth a dignified and handsome effect." He sought to make good

Plantings around "old" Old Main

on the development of blocks of buildings that had been established, and he suggested a quadrangle where Pattee, Sparks, and Burrowes are now. While the structure of the area is not quite the same today, its origins are very much present in spirit, especially in the plantings. Lowrie called for "shaded walks [and] . . . interesting terraces," a campus whose plantings and buildings suggested dignity and calm, an arrangement fitting in with late-nineteenth-century Romantic ideals. Interestingly, the document's conceptual painting of campus shows radii, drawn with trees, originating at Old Main and running to all ends of campus.

William Waring wanted shade, security, comfort, and a dignified appearance. However he anticipated what the rocky fields would become, he knew that trees and hedges would have to make it welcoming. Lowrie's terraces near Sparks and Burrowes were covered not with vines or statuary (both of which were suggested as possibilities) but with trees and hedges.

For the 1930s and 1940s, when Sparks Building and several other buildings were completed, Penn State had hired another landscape architect to furnish a comprehensive plan. Thomas W. Sears built on Lowrie's plan, adding his own flourish: plantings designed to soften the quadrangles and other building groupings. Introducing irregularly positioned trees and hedges would offset the otherwise rigid geometry the buildings created. Today, if you walk up to the library by way of the Mall and stand on the steps of Pattee prior to entering, you might smell the scent of French lilacs if it is April or May. They come from a hedge some nine feet tall, at the northern end of Sparks, tucked next to a decades-old hemlock and originally comprising thirteen varieties of lilac.

The first hedge plants were installed at the time construction of the building was finished, and for nearly seventy years that hedge has endured, had parts replanted, and maintained its spot. Planted as a result of Sears's plan, the plants embodied Waring's hedges, Lowrie's desire for geometry, and Sears's own desire for less rigid lines in the landscape. While the lilac hedge is planted in a line that parallels the north end of Sparks and the adjacent wall of West Pattee, its branches spill over the sidewalk, and its top mimics the tops of the trees visible all around. By doing so, the lilacs maintain the geometry while appearing less austere than would a formally clipped hedge. And as Waring would no doubt appreciate, it attracts birds throughout the year.

Today, two "overmature" American elms flank the front of Old Main. I learned several years ago that each tree was insured for over $20,000. So critical was the look of the elms to the identity of Penn State that they were assigned a hard and fast value. It's not surprising. Penn State conducted a survey four years ago in which it learned that alumni identify powerfully with a handful of images: the Nittany Lion, Joe Paterno, Old Main, and the elms. Penn State's American elm trees are the only plants on campus with their own specific endowment, provided as a gift from the Class of 1996. The elms are also the most imperiled plants on campus.

The oldest elms on campus—planted between 1890 and 1920—are at the end of their life cycle. Because of their size, around one hundred feet tall with branch spans even wider, and with their susceptibility to disease weakening their structure, the trees must be maintained and watched very carefully. A bad thunderstorm or early snowstorm can wreak havoc on the few elms left. In 2002, high winds tore down one of the massive elms behind Old Main, next to Schwab Auditorium. In November 1995, a sudden and ferocious snowstorm brought down 140 trees on campus, among them several elms. The elms not toppled altogether still lost limbs, and the day after the storm elm branches were stacked so deep on the Allen Street Mall that it was actually impossible to walk there. It was the biggest hit the elms had taken since 1950.

Fortunately, Penn State has supported a tree care program since at least the 1940s, and today the University Tree Commission, as well as other planning organizations, works to ensure that the campus remains green. The elms had long been well-maintained and pruned, such that only a blizzard like that of 1995 could do real damage, and even then was prevented from doing worse. Horticulturists at the University are also developing strains of American elm that can resist Dutch elm disease, so that dying and damaged trees may be replaced with plants more likely to withstand the disease.

Some elms have already been replaced, particularly in front of Schwab Auditorium, in what is called the Elm Management Area, the space between Burrowes Road and the Pugh Street mall, and from Pattee Library to College Avenue. Any elm lost or taken down in that area is replaced with another elm, while elms lost anywhere else (and there are few anywhere else) are replaced with lower-maintenance shade trees like locust, ash, hickory, or oak. That such a zone as the Elm Management Area exists reveals how integral the elms have become to campus identity. In 1997, Jeff Dice, then supervisor of grounds maintenance for the Office of the Physical Plant, estimated that while the elms made up less than 5 percent of the trees on campus, their maintenance required 42 percent of the arborists' time. Is it worth it?

Many alumni would give a resounding yes. But why? Consider the setup of some of the most memorable places on the University Park campus, conceived of as garden "rooms." Landscape architects, designers, and gardeners will all break a landscape up into units, as it is useful to think of spaces in terms of who inhabits them and uses them. While someone working on a residential landscape might conceive of "rooms" for play for a family with children, a dining area for alfresco eating, and a kitchen garden, for designing a garden on the scale of a campus, rooms might make more sense thought of as auditoriums, classrooms, or entries. For instance, the Mall is a long room connecting town with gown. Starting at what might be the spiritual center of town, the corner of College and Allen, the Mall ends at what is the academic core of the University, the library. So what ought such an entrance room look like? How should it be decorated to accommodate the expectations of students and returning alumni, visitors from all over the world, and the people who work in State College and the Centre Region?

It needs to be welcoming, covered in shade and grounded with wide walks and generous strips of lawn. The shade and the cool, flat lawns make it calm, and the trees themselves frame the points at either end of the room, Pattee and Paterno Libraries and Allen Street. On one end, gates, town, scurrying pedestrians, elms and locusts continue in rough congruity both up the hill and across the street, off into State College. At the other end, the pillars of Pattee echo the neighboring buildings, Sparks and Burrowes, as well as the tree trunks supporting the canopy. The Mall might even be read as a journey, from the concerns of work and daily life to the quiet, individual, and meditative process of reading, of communing with the mind. Could this effect be achieved without the presence of the cherished elms?

Consider how different, yet complementary, is the feel at the western end of campus, that portion dominated by the Information Sciences and Technology Building. It is the kind of building that students nickname: in 2003, its debut year, students dubbed it the Graham Span. Yet it is a rise of a building that, in its placement against the mountains behind it (if you approach from the north), approximates a dominant feature of the landscape. In fact, that approximation is one of the building's more controversial traits; because it blocks the mountains behind it, and then mimics them, some think the building inconsistent with the age-old vision for campus. In the Lowrie plan, he wrote specifically that campus

Pattee through the trees

plantings should provide and maintain "unobstructed outlooks" of the mountains and the campus.

Yet one might respond that, as Asian-influenced gardeners posit, landscapes can be viewed from many places, including from within buildings. From the IST building's windows, on one side you will see Atherton's serpentine approach, not unlike the building's gentle curve, as well as the mountains' undulating lines from the other. But perhaps most relevant, consider the plantings that surround it: trees, in different forms, a grove here, a line there, highlighting foot routes, clustering in corners, mimicking the leafy expanse of campus itself, softening the building's dominance with the greenery that, at one time, was all around where it now stands.

The Mall and the IST entrance are both referred to in the most current landscaping plan as "gateways," foyers writ large, lasting-impression kinds of places. Their prominence and importance says so much about what Penn State has become: a place that matters enough to the rest of the world that its gates must be among the most memorable places a person will experience. Thus, they need the height of trees, sweetened air, wide avenues, nothing that might even suggest narrow or cramped space.

Once within the gateways, the landscape changes. Walking across the IST bridge and into campus, you are again struck by the waiting wall of green. As well, the gates from the Class of 1903 stand at the head of a new pedestrian mall running eastward along Pollock Road toward the HUB. The route itself is flanked by trees that eventually join the march of trunks that make up Calder's walk. Old Main's tower is off to the right, atop the elms, and the leafy tops of Burrowes Road cross directly in front. On the right spring day, leaving the opening of the building, you will begin to smell the Koreanspice viburnums planted all along Pollock Road, tucked near West Halls, pressed up by Willard and Carnegie, growing near Old Main. While, again, they may not be the same actual plants, their presence dates from over a century ago.

Campus planners have torn up many buildings and roads in the 150 years of Penn State's existence, but have been careful nearly every time to preserve the larger idea that predated any given improvement. Around Sparks Building, despite additions and construction, the lilac hedge at the north end has been in existence for over seventy years. The Katsura trees and their delicate, heart-shaped leaves have shivered in the breeze since the building was first built, and while they haven't ever been replaced, the elms behind the building were. Even then, when American elms were sufficiently imperiled as to make replanting them, for a while, unwise, Penn State opted for *Zelcova serrata*, the so-called Chinese elm. While many think these are an aesthetically inferior tree compared to an American elm, they were the closest (and hardiest) visual analogue, and so were the best option for maintaining the basic look of a beloved space.

In 1946, Walter Trainer realized the growing complexity of Penn State's tree collection and so compiled *Campus Trees and Shrubs*, a census and schematic for finding and determining the identity of the five-hundred-plus species and varieties of trees and shrubs on campus at the time. In it, he articulates the result and the enhancement of Waring's initial ideas: "We are aware of the fact that one cannot enter the campus without being impressed by it's [*sic*] stately elms, oaks and maples that dominate the landscape." If his prose may be clunky, Trainer's awareness is nonetheless the guiding vision today. The campus has evolved from the laboratory it was conceived of in its early days and has become an ongoing work that adopts the most current thinking on the relationships between humans and their made and natural worlds.

Each year, I enjoy watching the men and women who prune the yews on campus. They often do so not with gas or electrical hedge trimmers, but with hand-held secateurs. They hold each branch and cut in such a way that, when they are finished, you see that the shrubs have been reduced in size, but they do not wear the obvious and severe signs of having been pruned. The workers prune the yews so as not to make their presence felt, so that the shrub maintains its natural aspect while still letting light within, turning the inside to green. The men and women who care for the yews also prune other trees and shrubs, and they are well trained. They know how, in the words of poet Len Roberts,

> a bird [can] fly
> through the limbs of a properly pruned
> tree
> without touching wood or bud.

Because of them, whatever landscape room you are in, you will not see the sins of strip-mall landscaping—greenery pruned into perverse, tight-branched clumps, trees left limb-stuffed and straggling amid concrete expanses, lawns choking up against buildings. You will instead see progres-

sion from building to lawn, zones filled with graduated levels of shrubs, vines, ground covers, and, increasingly, perennial flowering plants. And due to their efforts, you will feel the same coolness, security, and serenity on the lawns and under the trees that you once did as a student.

The University Park campus has many more "garden rooms" than those mentioned here. Hort Woods, or North Woods—located between the Arts and Forum buildings and Park Avenue—is just as contrived a space as the malls, a fact many are surprised to hear, despite the obviously planned serpentine path and benches contained within the trees. Originally an uncut plot of trees dating back before the founding of the University, a horticulture professor later added several trees there to make a larger forest-like tract, seeking to provide an appropriate backdrop to the buildings on what was once Ag Hill. Today, strolling in yet another room, under the two enormous beeches or near the unusual willow oak beside Weaver Building, you can readily see the mark of planning: many of the younger trees have plaques, explaining who planted the tree and why, as so many are memorials. The landscape has meant so much to some alumni that their relatives felt it necessary to include their memory as a part of it.

The gesture also ensures that the memory will become part of something larger and ever changing. The campus is a place of neither permanence nor rigidity. Each December and May, we are reminded of this fact by the departure of several thousand students. Throughout the year, employees move in and out, families settle in or leave the area, and faculty move on to other places, sometimes returning, sometimes not. The same is true of the physical character of Penn State. While many alumni consider Old Main a quintessential piece of Penn State, the current building is relatively young, dating back to 1930. The elms? The oldest ones are at least forty years younger than the university.

The campus is perhaps on the cusp of its greatest surge of landscape growth since Waring's days. The Hintz Alumni Gardens, the medieval garden, the sustainability garden by Old Botany, and the Arboretum are currently in development. Scores of planters overflowing with flowering annuals are one of the most conspicuous additions to campus in recent years, and perennial beds have appeared over the last decade. While the new developments in the campus environment reflect how much has changed, it is still instructive to walk through the campus on a Saturday morning in February. Bundle up, have a cup of coffee, and walk. Look around. See the bare trees, the straight stone terraces, the gnarled twists within the hedges. Look at the bones of campus, see how little has changed, how what remains in winter, in the cold, in the darkest months of the year, when little else moves, is still the same. Strange as it may sound, take comfort in that landscape. It shows what endures.

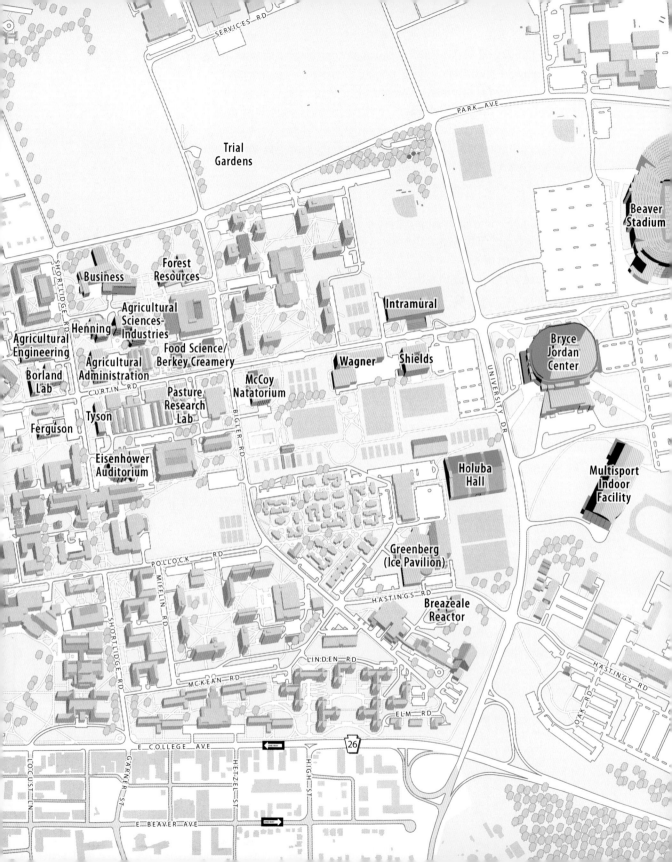

EAST CAMPUS

Eisenhower Auditorium · Agricultural Sciences Complex

Smeal College of Business Building · School of Forest Resources Building

Athletic Facilities · Shields/Wagner Buildings

Bryce Jordan Center · Beaver Stadium · Innovation Park

Commencement exercises, Future Farmers of America conferences, lectures, religious services, musical performances, theatre, and dance: Eisenhower Auditorium holds it all. With seating for an audience of 2,600, Eisenhower is Penn State's primary space for performing arts groups and presents nearly two hundred events annually. One of only nine buildings on campus constructed during the 1970s, Eisenhower opened in 1974 as the University Auditorium and in 1977 took the name of University president Milton Eisenhower (1950–56). The hall's inaugural performances featured the Pittsburgh Symphony Orchestra. Designed by Sanders and Bicksler in collaboration with Bolt, Beranek, and Newman, Eisenhower Auditorium represents part of a larger effort to create a "modern arts complex" at Penn State in the 1970s and to encourage students, alumni, and the public to take an interest in a "broad spectrum of the arts."

The auditorium currently houses Penn State's Center for the Performing Arts (CPA), which itself grew out of the Artists Series begun in the late 1950s—a series that intended to enrich students' education through the arts and, later, through a lecture series. Most Artists Series programs appeared in Schwab Auditorium or Rec Hall until the new auditorium opened. With the newly expanded space came a broader range of programming, including musicals from Broadway, family shows, and the like. In 1985, the CPA moved its offices to Eisenhower Auditorium.

The CPA strives to present diverse programs, from the well-loved to the experimental. During the 2003–4 season, Eisenhower Auditorium hosted a number of musicals—including *The Music Man*, *Miss Saigon*, *Kiss Me Kate*, and *The Sound of Music*—as well as performances by such groups as the Newport Jazz Festival, the Royal Philharmonic Orchestra, and Opera Verdi Europa. Productions of *Othello* and *The Nutcracker* have appeared on the Eisenhower stage, as have the Wynton Marsalis Septet, a Siberian dance company, West

African drummers, the Dayton Contemporary Dance Company, a troupe of Chinese acrobats, and vocalist Linda Eder. Eisenhower remains the primary venue for Penn State's Distinguished Speakers series as well. Past speakers have included Bob Woodward, Maya Angelou, the late Christopher Reeve, James Earl Jones, and Elie Wiesel, among many others.

• • • • •

What Bugs You at PSU

In 1937, Stuart Frost was hired to teach entomology at Penn State and, in addition to his classroom duties, he quickly established the College's first organized collection of insects. The museum, which is now housed in Headhouse III on Curtin Road, was named for Frost in 1969 and is now recognized as holding one of the leading regional insect collections on the East Coast.

The museum's collection includes insects from 15,000 different species and contains a total of more than 700,000 individual specimens. Some of the specimens still on display date back to Frost's first days collecting insects in the early 1900s, when he was a teenager. The Frost Museum seeks to cater to insect enthusiasts at every level: the curator and staff maintain exhibits for the general public and presentations for visiting grade school groups, as shown here, while the museum's accommodating loan policies allow dedicated scholars to use the collection for research.

The Frost Museum takes seriously its mission to transform the public's perception of insects from icky to interesting. It offers many educational events and programs, including the wildly popular Great Insect Fair and Children's Bug Camp, as well as Penn State's own answer to crime scene investigation, the annual Forensic Entomology Workshop.

Borland Laboratory (1932, renovated in 1959, 1961, 1965, 1970) | Agricultural Engineering (1940) | Agricultural Administration (1972) | Henning Building (1966) | Agricultural Sciences and Industries (1991) | Ferguson Building (1938) | Tyson Building (1949) | Food Science Building (2005)

Since its founding as Farmers' High School in 1855, Penn State has been shaped by the study and practice of agriculture. In 1861, Penn State became the first American college to offer a baccalaureate degree in agriculture, and after the passage of the Morrill Land-Grant Act of 1862, Penn State became the exclusive land-grant college of the Commonwealth. In 1874, as the curriculum broadened and enrollment numbers grew, the Agricultural College was renamed The Pennsylvania State College.

Today, the northeast part of campus is home to a cluster of agricultural science buildings in an area known as Ag Hill. Penn State's College of Agricultural Sciences now is the sixth largest agricultural college in the nation and the largest in the Big Ten. The original Ag Hill complex, which included the Agricultural Experiment Station building and barns, was built in the late nineteenth century, with a major addition between 1899 and 1906. In the 1930s, money from the federal Public Works Administration allowed for the construction of Agricultural Engineering and Ferguson buildings and the Poultry Plant, which has since been razed. The federal Pasture Research Lab, a facility of the U.S. Department of Agriculture, entered the scene in the 1930s as well, as did Borland Laboratory. More recent decades have seen slower but still-steady growth: Henning in 1966, Agricultural Administration in the 1970s, and Agricultural Sciences and Industries, completed in 1991. The new Food Science building, set to open in 2006, will include laboratories, classrooms, and a state-of-the-art processing facility, as well as the Berkey Creamery.

One remnant of Penn State's earliest days in agricultural education is the Dairy Barn watering trough, located near the corner of Shortlidge and Curtin roads. It was originally located in the open court area of the old Dairy Barn, pictured opposite, which was built in 1914. The Penn State Dairy Science Club and the College of Agriculture Alumni Association restored the trough and relocated it in 1972. The old buildings—and new—on Ag Hill testify to the continued importance of Penn State's founding field.

· · · · ·

How Does Our Garden Grow?

Patches of breathtaking color decorate Bigler Road at its intersection with Park Avenue—the site of Penn State's trial gardens. Established in the 1930s, the trial garden program has scrutinized thousands of annual and perennial flowers and vegetables, evaluating their performance for the horticulture industry as well as for the gardening public. Flower enthusiasts, such as those pictured here, have visited the gardens for decades to appreciate the blooms. The adjacent medieval gardens, constructed with funding from AT&T and based on tapestries and paintings from the Middle Ages, include a kitchen garden, a pleasure ground boasting hollyhocks, Sweet William, and an enclosed contemplation garden, as well as exhibits of other medieval crops and fruit trees.

Surprisingly, the Smeal College of Business began as an outgrowth of an entirely different part of the University: the College of the Liberal Arts. In the first half of the twentieth century, one component of Liberal Arts was the Department of Commerce and Finance (C&F, dismissed as "Cuties and Fun" by some). But despite the moniker, the department pushed to be taken seriously, and by the mid-1920s, C&F represented more than half of the enrollment in the College of the Liberal Arts. In 1953, as part of a national trend to improve the quality of business education, Penn State founded the College of Business Administration. In 1989, the College was named for Mary Jean and Frank P. Smeal, whose gift of $10 million showed the depth of their support for management education.

The College of Business now comprises six academic departments—Accounting, Finance, Insurance and Real Estate, Management and Organization, Marketing, and Supply Chain and Information Systems. Under Dean Judy Olian, the College has renewed its MBA program and has launched a number of educational initiatives. Among these is a technologically advanced laboratory—the trading room—that brings "the reality of Wall Street to the University Park campus," as students learn about financial markets around the world, stock trading, options, and other aspects of the global economy.

In 2005, the College moved to a new building (designed by Robert A. M. Stern/Bower Lewis Thrower Architects) that now houses all of its departments, research centers, and staff. At 210,000 square feet, the building (pictured here) will be Penn State's largest academic facility and features a four-story glass atrium, the trading room, classrooms, student commons areas, a café, an auditorium, and an outdoor plaza.

Trees are ubiquitous on the University Park campus—but they are rarely seen dangling from the raised arm of a crane! Still, visitors to University Park in December 2004 might have noticed just such an unusually located tree near the intersection of Park Avenue and Bigler Road. A longstanding tradition among builders calls for a small tree to be placed atop the frame of a new building once the structural steel has been set in place. The School of Forest Resources observed this custom, with a twist, when it chose a thirty-foot-tall Douglas fir tree—grown as part of the school's research into improved varieties of Christmas trees—as the "topping-off tree" for its new building.

The School of Forest Resources (SFR) was established at the University Park campus in 1907. After absorbing the State Forest Academy (founded in 1903 by Joseph Rothrock), it added programs of study in wood products in 1941 and in wildlife and fisheries science in 1981. The SFR also manages more than 8,000 acres of forestlands for research, education, and outreach, including Stone Valley Forest in Huntingdon County.

With the opening of the new four-story SFR Building in late 2005, all of the departments within the School of Forest Resources will be united under one roof for the first time. The building features a number of teaching and research laboratories; technologically advanced classrooms; the Schatz Tree Genetics Center; outreach facilities; and the 150-seat Steimer Auditorium.

The SFR Building incorporates Pennsylvania hardwoods into its design: four red maple laminated beams serve as primary roof supports for the glassed-in atrium. Other hardwoods from the Commonwealth form part of the paneling as well as the seating areas, and a pleasant outdoor garden features native plants. The building also adheres to the principles of Leadership in Energy and Environmental Design, promoting and raising awareness of "green" building practices.

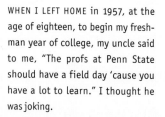

WHEN I LEFT HOME in 1957, at the age of eighteen, to begin my freshman year of college, my uncle said to me, "The profs at Penn State should have a field day 'cause you have a lot to learn." I thought he was joking.

Two chance happenings at Penn State profoundly affected my college days and life. I was in gym class freshman year when the instructor, Norm Gordon, timed us running. After class he asked me to try out for track. I thought about thirty seconds and said, "Sure. Next spring I'll give it a try." Gordon bellowed, "Next spring?! We have an indoor meet at the Naval Academy in a month. This is a Division I sports program!" I didn't know that there was indoor track and I hadn't followed sports enough to know about NCAA divisions. I tried out, made the team, was undefeated in the quarter-mile in dual and triangular meets my senior year, and set a Penn State indoor 440-yard record that stood for fourteen years. Not bad for a student athlete who had

37 ATHLETIC FACILITIES

Greenberg Sports Complex (1954; renovated 1962, 1980) | Holuba Hall (1986) | Multisport Indoor Facility (1999) | McCoy Natatorium (1969) | Intramural Building (1975)

Beaver Stadium is certainly the most visible sports structure on campus, but it is by no means the only one. The football offices are housed in the Greenberg Sports Complex on the eastern side of campus. The complex also holds one of Penn State's most popular athletics facilities, the Ice Pavilion, where University and community hockey teams practice and compete. Containing both the main rink and a smaller "studio" rink for skating lessons and private parties, the Ice Pavilion is open to the public throughout the year.

Holuba Hall, one of the largest prefabricated metal buildings in the country, is an indoor athletic facility used by several varsity sports teams. Built in 1986, the hall was named one year later for Stanley Holuba and his family, who donated $1 million for its construction. The 118,000-square-foot facility includes an 80-by-120-yard Astroturf field and four-lane track. Holuba Hall sits adjacent to an outdoor football practice field.

Across University Drive from Holuba Hall stands the Multisport Indoor Facility. Built in 1999, the building is divided into two main spaces: the Box and the Program Building. The Box houses a 200-meter track, 56-yard Astroturf field, weight training room, and spectator stands, while the Program Building contains offices and locker rooms. The Multisport Indoor Facility, like Holuba Hall (pictured below), utilizes cost-effective low-intensity infrared heating. To cool such a large space, the natural winds are utilized for cross-ventilation, due to the building's location in a valley adjacent to the Bryce Jordan Center. (In the winter, sledding enthusiasts flock to this slope.)

McCoy Natatorium, near East Halls, was built in 1969 and is named for Ernest B. McCoy, Penn State's director of athletics and dean of the College of Health, Physical Education, and Recreation between 1952 and 1970. At first glance, the facility's two six-lane pools look similar, but they serve very different purposes. The twenty-five-meter instructional pool is shallow and warm, designed for those taking lessons, undergoing therapy, or just seeking relaxation. The twenty-five-yard competition pool is twice as deep (ten feet at the deep end) and is heated only to a cool seventy-nine degrees. This is the pool used for training by serious lap swimmers. The diving well, with a water depth of fourteen feet, boasts one- and three-meter springboards. The Natatorium's largest pool is a fifty-meter Olympic-size outdoor pool. Here lap swimmers and sunbathers exercise or relax on summer days, and adventurous types plunge from the ten-meter diving platform.

When the Intramural Building (designed by Sanders and Bicksler) officially opened to students on September 4, 1975, it was the culmination of a

never seen or ran in a meet until he was eighteen years old.

The second chance happening occurred in 1961. A friend asked me at lunch what I was going to do about my military draft status. He got me to talk to the Marine recruiter at the HUB at 1:00 P.M. that same day. I passed the officer selection test, raised my right hand for the oath, and made my 2:00 P.M. class. I had just signed up for four years in the U.S. Marine Corps. I didn't know one could get a commission without taking ROTC, but a quick decision on campus had steered me in the right direction. (I didn't know how to tell my parents I had enlisted, so I didn't! They only found out when the FBI went to my high school, where my brother John [PSU Class of '58] was a teacher.) Those Marine years turned out to be the best and most rewarding work years of my forty-year career, after my time at Penn State.

—GEORGE F. METZGAR, CLASS OF '61

decade-long undertaking. In March 1965, Penn State inaugurated a large addition to Rec Hall (including such amenities as the squash and handball annex). At the unveiling ceremony, C. M. "Dutch" Sykes, director of the Division of Recreational Sports, was already trying to sell University administrators on the idea of a completely new athletic facility for undergraduates. Sykes was concerned that Rec Hall was inconveniently located, especially for students living in East Halls, and that Rec Hall's availability to students would diminish as it was increasingly used to host concerts, meetings, and "Nobel Prize orators." Sykes contributed at every step of the venture, from drafting the initial proposal to the administration to a last-minute suggestion that the name be changed from the Student Recreation Building to the Intramural Building, and his hard work has been enjoyed by students ever since.

Scattered throughout the campus are many other athletic facilities, including seventeen lighted football fields, twenty-three softball fields, six lighted soccer fields, a rugby field, a Frisbee team area, ten basketball courts, fifty-six outdoor and four indoor tennis courts (including the outdoor courts pictured on page 124), and two eighteen-hole golf courses.

• • • • •

Penn State's Nuclear Year: 1955

In 1955, Penn State became the first university in the United States to own and operate an AEC-licensed nuclear reactor. That same year, across campus in Osmond Laboratory, Professor Erwin Mueller was using a field ion microscope of his own design to make him the first person to "see" the atom.

The Breazeale Reactor was named for Penn State's first professor of nuclear engineering, William M. Breazeale, and was built as part of Dwight Eisenhower's Atoms for Peace initiative, which aimed to find constructive uses for nuclear power. Part of the Radiation Science and Engineering Center and the Nuclear Engineering Program's major experimental facility, Breazeale is a research reactor, used not for producing electricity but as a laboratory for studying nuclear physics and chemistry.

As an undergraduate student in 1972, Jackie Scheurin Tate became the first woman to be licensed as a reactor operator.

38 SHIELDS BUILDING (1967) / WAGNER BUILDING (1958; MAJOR RENOVATIONS 1965, 1977)

Although Shields Building (designed by Halheimer and Weitz) sits tucked away at the northeast corner of the campus, it contains many of the most important undergraduate offices in the University, including those of Administrative Information Services, Housing and Food Services, the Bursar, Student Aid, Undergraduate Admissions, and the University Registrar. For decades after its opening in 1967, Shields saw thousands of students pass through every semester in order to conduct the business of their educations. In recent years, with students able to do everything from class registration to meal-plan adjustment on the Internet, the days of standing in long lines at various counters in Shields to apply for dorm housing or financial aid are gone. But despite the increased reliance on electronic transactions, Shields remains home to the core administrative offices.

The Wagner Building, designed by the General State Authority, has been long known as "the ROTC building." Wagner houses the offices of the campus's Navy, Army, and Air Force Reserve Officers' Training Corps (ROTC), and it was named in honor of H. Edward Wagner, a Penn State graduate and United States Army lieutenant killed in France in 1944. Beginning in 1965,

Wagner had also been home to one of the most visible and community-oriented aspects of Penn State: the University's public broadcasting stations. The radio station WPSU and the public television station WPSX (now WPSU-TV) both ran their main production facilities from the unassuming brick rectangle until their move to Innovation Park.

39 BRYCE JORDAN CENTER (1996)

Courtesy the Bryce Jordan Center

University president Bryce Jordan took office in 1983 with a clear goal in mind: to make Penn State one of the ten best public research universities in the country. The most prominent testament to his success, perhaps, is the $55 million Bryce Jordan Center.

Ground was broken for the Jordan Center in December 1993 under the watch of Jordan's successor, Joab Thomas. Predictably, such a massive undertaking was not without setbacks; in particular, an unusually harsh winter delayed building for several months. So bleak was the situation at one point that Indiana University basketball coach Bobby Knight declared that it would take a "construction company from Mars" to complete the Center on schedule. But the builders proved Knight wrong, and on January 6, 1996, barely two years after groundbreaking, the Bryce Jordan Center opened to the public.

The Jordan Center covers 360,000 square feet—more than eight acres—and can seat 16,000 spectators. In addition to its main arena, the building includes conference rooms, banquet facilities, and 140 offices. With the exception of swimming and football, the offices of all Penn State athletics departments are housed in the Center.

Though the raw materials that make up the Center are impressive—3,100 tons of structural steel, 26,000 cubic yards of concrete, plus another 5,600 tons of concrete seating—even more impressive are the ways in which the University has managed to use them. The Jordan Center was conceived as a multipurpose venue, one that would, in the words of Penn State administrator Bill McKinnon, "become a civic center for the middle of this state. We wanted to build a facility that not only served the University's needs, but also the region's needs." Events at the Jordan Center are thus quite diverse, ranging from NCAA basketball, commencement ceremonies, stand-up comedy, children's shows, and a homebuilders' expo to appearances by political activists and concerts by musicians including Elton John (pictured opposite), the Dave Matthews Band, Garth Brooks, Cher, Sarah Brightman, and Metallica, as well as WWF wrestling and monster truck shows.

• • • • •

Lady Lions Roar

For women's sports at Penn State, 1964 was an important year. It featured the University's first official intercollegiate events in women's golf, fencing, gymnastics, field hockey, and the women's sport for which Penn State has become best known: basketball. Since that very first game—and win—against Bloomsburg University, the Lady Lions basketball team has maintained a consistent standard of excellence, with only two losing seasons in more than four decades. For many years the Lady Lions called Rec Hall home, but in January 1996 both the men's and women's basketball teams moved across campus to the newly completed Bryce Jordan Center. With an average of 7,000 spectators per game, and record attendance levels exceeding 12,000, the Lady Lions and their fans can be glad that the team now has a home venue large enough to accommodate the ever-growing popularity of women's basketball at Penn State. Pictured here is Penn State and Big Ten leading scorer Kelly Mazzante.

40 BEAVER STADIUM (BEAVER FIELD 1893; NEW BEAVER FIELD 1909; AT CURRENT LOCATION 1960; MOST RECENT MAJOR RENOVATION COMPLETED 2001)

WE WERE AN independent-minded and sometimes unpolished, poverty-level group of students proudly wearing parts of our World War II uniforms. Many of us had never hoped for a college education. Yet here it was, on a silver platter, as partial payment for fighting a war we firmly believed was necessary and just. (How times change.)

As a group, we were older than the usual breed of college student and we created unique problems for some upper classmates, professors, and administrators. We had "been around" and were not about to conform to the usual traditions such as observing curfews, wearing dinks, and learning the Penn State cheers or the words to the alma mater.

Orientation week was a shambles and some of us didn't even show up. We were too busy getting in another week of summer work or finding a drafty low-rent attic room within walking distance of the campus. Most of us spent our freshman years at State Teachers Colleges across the Commonwealth while the main campus braced for our onslaught.

For visitors standing in the shadow of the current Beaver Stadium, it takes a significant leap of imagination to return to the late nineteenth century, when football games at Penn State were played on the lawn of Old Main. The first permanent campus home for football games was Old Beaver Field, located between Osmond and Frear laboratories; a blue historical marker commemorates the spot today. Beaver Field featured seating for a mere five hundred spectators, and the first game played there was in November 1893 against Western University of Pittsburgh (later to become the University of Pittsburgh). A larger arena, New Beaver Field, was dedicated in 1909. It became the home field for the Nittany Lions through the 1959 season and eventually seated thirty thousand. (Well more than a decade later, Rec Hall was built adjacent to New Beaver Field.) In 1960, the stadium was dismantled, moved to the east side of campus, and reassembled. Sixteen thousand seats were added in the process, and Beaver Stadium was complete. The stadium was dedicated in September 1960 with a win against Boston University; pictured here is a packed house from this era of the stadium's life.

Beaver Stadium has since seen numerous renovations and expansions, and with 107,282 seats, it remains the second-largest stadium in the Big Ten Confer-

ence—only Michigan Stadium is larger—and the fourth largest in the nation. The most recent expansion, begun in November 1999 at a cost of $93 million, involved adding a second deck in the south end zone, an east-side pavilion with enclosed suites, and a club-level seating section and stadium club, the Mount Nittany Lounge. The stadium's infrastructure saw significant improvements as well. An overflow crowd of 109,313 attended the Penn State–Miami game on September 1, 2001, the first in the newly expanded stadium.

Early 2002 saw the opening of another addition to Beaver Stadium: the All-Sports Museum. The museum, a noted tourist attraction, celebrates Penn State athletes and coaches and features photographs, memorabilia, equipment, and uniforms from past and present. Visitors to the museum can enjoy a variety of interactive exhibits, watch video presentations, see an assortment of athletic awards won by Penn Staters, including an Olympic gold medal—and even hold a football from the turn of the century.

Far above the southwest corner of Beaver Stadium—at 110 feet—hovers a copper-plated weathervane in the shape of the Nittany Lion. Commissioned by University trustee Joel N. Myers and sculpted by Travis Tuck, the weathervane measures ten feet in length, three feet in width, and nine feet in height and weighs in at about two thousand pounds.

· · · · ·

Got Meat?

Most Penn Staters are probably unaware that the best place on campus—and perhaps in town—to get a steak, lamb chops, or a pork tenderloin is the Penn State Meats Laboratory, located on Porter Road across from Beaver Stadium. On most Fridays during the fall and spring semesters, this meat processing facility operates a retail outlet for high-quality foods related to its primary mission: support of meats teaching, research, and extension for the Department of Dairy and Animal Science (College of Agricultural Sciences).

Built in 1958, the 16,000-square-foot structure has over 1,200 square feet of refrigerated space and is equipped to do most types of commercial meat processing, including sawing, grinding, chopping, macerating, injecting, massaging, cooking, smoking, and packing. The building also houses classrooms, faculty and staff offices, and research labs.

Classrooms were another revelation—to both students and professors. We asked questions. Boy, did we ask questions! Some startled professors found themselves defending their pronouncements and theories with new vigor. Many of us, along with the professors, were not certain that we were really college material. So we tried harder and most of us made it.

I believe our goals were primarily materialistic and our concerns for the social ills and injustices of the world were limited. We wanted to graduate, get a job, and get on with our interrupted lives.

We were the GI Bill men and women of the Class of 1950. Penn State survived our invasion. We still believe we were one of the best investments the government ever made.

—JACK McMILLAN, CLASS OF '50

Strike Up the Blue Band!

It was the use of music in student military training at Penn State that led to the establishment of the Cadet Bugle Corps (pictured here in 1899), the Blue Band's precursor, initiated by student George H. Deike in 1899. A donation from steel magnate and Board of Trustees member Andrew Carnegie made possible the formation of a full brass band in the summer of 1901. By 1913, the organization was known as the College Band, and the first permanent director of bands, Wilfred O. "Tommy" Thompson, was appointed in 1914.

The name "Blue Band" was first used in 1923 to signify a formation of blue-uniformed band members surrounded by a larger, brown-uniformed group. This select group became Penn State's official traveling marching band. Eventually, all band members wore blue, and the name stuck.

For more on the Blue Band, see The Penn State Blue Band: A Century of Pride and Precision, by Thomas E. Range II and Sean Patrick Smith (Penn State Press).

The Blue Band numbers almost three hundred members, including musicians, silks, majorettes, the drum major, and the Blue Sapphire (the featured twirler). With the October 24, 2004, dedication of the Blue Band building, located adjacent to the Blue Band practice field at University Drive and Services Road, the band gained a 6,000-square-foot indoor rehearsal room, plus instrument and uniform storage space, locker rooms, staff offices, and showcases for Blue Band memorabilia. No more soggy feet or frozen toes for the Blue Band—at least not during rehearsal!

• • • • •

"You Say JOEPA, I Say TERNO! JOEPA [clap-clap] TERNO!"

At twenty-three years old, Joseph Vincent Paterno became Penn State's assistant coach under Rip Engle, a position he held for sixteen years. Harry Truman was president and the Dodgers were still in Brooklyn. Much in the world has changed since 1950, of course, but Paterno's leadership and work ethic both on and off the field have remained steady and strong. Between 1968 and 1994, the Penn State Nittany Lions football team had five perfect seasons and won two national championships. Evidence of Paterno's commitment to the scholar-athlete and his dedication to academics can be found throughout the university, most notably in the high graduation rates among athletes and the Paterno family library philanthropies. In 2008, God willing, JoePa will surpass Amos Alonzo Stagg's record forty-one seasons with the University of Chicago as head football coach.

Eleven men preceded Joe Paterno as head coach of the Nittany Lions.

George Hoskins	1889–95	Bill Hollenback	1909, 1911–14
Samuel Newton	1896–99	Jack Hollenback	1910
Sam Boyle	1899	Dick Harlow	1915–17
Pop Golden	1900–1902	Hugo Bezdek	1918–29
Dan Reed	1903	Rip Engle	1950–65
Tom Fennell	1904–8	Joe Paterno	1966–present

• • • • •

Nittany Lion Football Historical Highlights: The First Hundred Years (or So)

November 12, 1881	Students organized the first football game against the University of Lewisburg (later renamed Bucknell University). In freezing drizzle and with no administrative support, The Pennsylvania State College won, 9-0. Bucknell remained State's bitter rival for many years.
September 1887	Freshman George "Lucy" Linsz helped organize the first official football team for the College. Lucy even supplied the first football.
November 12, 1887	State won its first official game—against Bucknell—54-0.
November 11, 1889	With only nine players available to play, Penn State lost, 106-0, to Lehigh. The referee took pity and stopped the game with five minutes left.
September 1897	The first helmet used in Penn State football was introduced at practice by "Henny" Scholl. Made from a derby with the brim cut off and rags stuffed inside for padding, it got little actual use.
October 24, 1903	State beat Pitt in their first meeting, 59-6—a margin of victory that stood for sixty-five years. Carl Forkum scored 39 points.
November 16, 1912	In the first game between Penn State and Ohio State, the Lions scored 37, the Buckeyes 0. But because the Buckeyes walked off the

I WASN'T A great high school athlete; in fact, I couldn't even make the varsity football team when we only had forty-four boys in the entire school. I decided at that point that my future was being a sports announcer. My idol in the early 1940s was Bill Stern, the Jim McKay of his time. Arriving at Penn State in June 1945, as a very green freshman, I approached the publicity director, Jim Coogan, and the alumni director, Ridge Riley, as to whether there might be a job for me in the Press Box; of course, I was hoping to "spot players" for the radio announcer. Unfortunately, I learned that job was done for years by our terrific gymnastics coach, Gene Wettstone. However, they would find something for me to do. When football season approached, I received a pass that got me into the sanctuary known as the Press Box.

The first year I worked on statistics, recording each play, and tabulating yards gained per player, or the number of tackles per player, etc. That job was okay, but what was exciting was the display of food, freely available to anyone in the Press Box, and for a rapidly growing kid, this was *heaven*. The next year I did spot players for the public-address announcer, and that's far tougher than on radio, since the fans could see all of your mistakes. I did get asked to make one trip, to Bucknell, at which game I invited my dad to check my accuracy.

	field with nine minutes to go, charging "unnecessary roughness" against the Lions, the official score was recorded as a 1-0 forfeit.
October 25, 1914	Harvard's twenty-two-game winning streak was stopped by Penn State with a 13-13 tie at Cambridge. Two days later, a bonfire exploded at the campus celebration, injuring many and causing major damage to school buildings.
October 9, 1920	At the first alumni Homecoming Day game, Penn State beat Dartmouth, 14-7, in front of a record crowd of 12,000.
January 1, 1923	Penn State played in the Rose Bowl, its first postseason bowl appearance. The Lions lost to Southern California, 14-7, but received $21,350 for participating.
November 28, 1931	State beat Lehigh 31-0, ending a seven-game losing streak and closing out the season with a 2-8 record, the worst in the team's history.
November 13, 1937	State beat Maryland, 21-14, at Beaver Field, achieving the team's first winning season since 1929.
October 1, 1938	The Penn State radio network was established and broadcast its first game, the home opener, with Penn State beating Maryland, 38-0.
November 20, 1938	Penn State finished with a 3-4-1 record as the team lost to Pitt, 26-0. This was the Lions' last losing season for forty-nine years, although the team managed to set three NCAA defensive records in 1938, one of which stands today—fewest yards allowed passing, 13.1 (105 yards in eight games).
September 1941	Brothers Dave Alston and Harry Alston of Midland, Pennsylvania, became the first African American members of the football team.
November 30, 1942	With a 6-1-1 record, Penn State gained Associated Press national ranking for the first time, tying at #19 with Minnesota and Holy Cross.
November 17, 1945	Wally Triplett took the field as the first African American to start in a Penn State game.
November 9, 1946	Miami University officials requested that for their November 29 meeting in Miami, Penn State leave African American team members Wally Triplett and Dennie Hoggard at home. Penn State canceled the game.
November 22, 1947	By beating Pitt 29-0, the '47 Lions became the first team in Penn State history to be undefeated in the regular season (9-0).

December 8, 1947	Penn State finished at #4, according to Associated Press rankings, and was awarded the Lambert Trophy as the best team in the East (an honor the team received twenty-four more times between 1961 and 1998). The team set defensive records for fewest rushing yards allowed per game—17 (153 yards in 9 games)—and fewest yards per rush—0.64 (153 yards in 240 rushes). Both records remain unbeaten.
May 27, 1950	Rip Engle hired Joe Paterno and assigned him to coach quarterbacks.
November 13, 1953	The Lions rallied from a 14-6 second-quarter deficit to beat Rutgers, 54-26, as they played their first game as The Pennsylvania State University.

My third year I had a variety of assignments, but the most prized one was the request to spot players for the television announcer doing the PSU-Navy game at Baltimore. It was in November 1947, and that was the season we were undefeated, tying SMU in the Cotton Bowl. We were national champions in our estimation. The morning of the game, it rained and snowed, creating a quagmire on the field. The numbers on the jerseys were soon obliterated, but based on three years attending many practice sessions, I knew each player by his movement and shape. With the help of binoculars from the top of Municipal Stadium, I was able to call most of the plays correctly, and even though it was a televised game, no viewer could possibly have detected my mistakes.

By this time, I was nearing graduation with a degree in chemical engineering. My experience in the Press Box convinced me that my career in engineering would probably be more successful than being a sports announcer, but I still recall with tremendous pleasure those Press Box experiences, and that included the most food I have ever eaten at a football game. Now I know why I grew seven inches in height during those three years in Nittany Valley.

—WALT ROBB, CLASS OF '48

THE STUFF OF "urban legends," every fall the rumor ran through the University Park campus that psychic Jeane Dixon had predicted that an ax murder would occur on Halloween night on the top floor of a high-rise women's dorm "in the largest dormitory complex at a major East Coast university." In the fall of 1981, residents of Tener and Brumbaugh Halls in East Halls—the largest women's high-rise dorms in the largest dorm complex at Penn State University—took those rumors to heart. It seemed to us that the prediction would actually come true! A sudden power outage one Halloween night left portions of East Halls in the dark. My fellow tenth-floor Tener residents and I scurried about lighting candles and shrieking, nervously making the trek down the ten flights of stairs, only to find that the power had gone out not because of a nefarious ax murderer but because a water main had broken in Parking Lot 80 and had flooded critical power facilities. Power was restored later that evening but the frayed nerves, bad dreams, and sleepless nights lasted a lot longer!

—JOAN EVERETT LAIMAN,
CLASSES OF '83 AND '85

October 19, 1957	Pete Mauthe, captain of the 1912 team, became the first Penn State player to be inducted into the College Football Hall of Fame.
September 17, 1960	22,559 fans watched the Lions beat Boston University, 20-0, in the first game played at Beaver Stadium.
October 3, 1960	To help alleviate traffic jams, Centre Daily Times editor Jerry Weinstein suggested that fans opt for picnic lunches before and picnic suppers after games—later referred to as "tailgating."
February 19, 1966	University president Eric Walker named Joe Paterno, thirty-eight, as head football coach, at an annual salary of $20,000.
December 7, 1968	After beating Syracuse, 30-12, the Lions finished the regular season undefeated (11-0) for the first time since 1947.
January 1, 1970	After the team's second unbeaten season, State beat Missouri, 10-3, in the Orange Bowl, a postseason venue chosen over the Cotton Bowl. President Richard Nixon delivered the national championship to Texas, the winner of the Cotton Bowl, touching off a bitter controversy.
December 13, 1973	John Cappelletti became the first Penn State player to win a Heisman Trophy.
November 13, 1978	Penn State was voted #1 in the Associated Press and United Press International polls for the first time in the team's ninety-one-year history.
October 20, 1981	Penn State was voted #1 after beating Syracuse, 41–16.
January 1, 1983	Penn State beat #1 Georgia in the Sugar Bowl to win the national championship.
September 8, 1984	84,409 fans were on hand as the "Wave" made its first appearance at Beaver Stadium.
January 2, 1987	Penn State upset #1 Miami, 14-10, in the Fiesta Bowl, winning its second national championship.
December 19, 1989	The Big Ten Conference extended Penn State an "invitation in principle" to join.

Penn State in the Pink

In the fall of 1887, a three-member committee representing sophomore, junior, and senior classes unanimously chose dark pink and black as the school colors. But—according to legend—problems arose when the pink in the baseball team's uniforms faded to white after several weeks' exposure to the sun. The students then opted for blue, rather than black, and white. The new blue-and-white color scheme was officially announced on March 18, 1890.

41 INNOVATION PARK (1994)

Located at a few miles' distance from the main campus of University Park, Innovation Park is, according to its mission statement, "the place where collaboration between the University and private sector companies can grow." Of Innovation Park's $440 million budget in 2002, $75 million came from industry-sponsored research. In addition to University offices, such as those of the Materials Research Institute and the Technology Center and Penn State Public Broadcasting, Innovation Park houses offices for more than twenty-five corporations, from the biomedical firm NanoHorizons to the Daybridge Child Development Center, which also provides child care for University employees. Special facilities at Innovation Park include a business incubator for fledgling companies and a class-10 cleanroom, which provides the dust-free environment necessary to build

delicate electronics. Although central Pennsylvania is not traditionally considered a major business hub, Innovation Park's leaders laud its location at the intersection of I-99 and U.S. Route 322, near the State College airport, as one of its favorable features.

One of the most important components of Innovation Park is the Penn Stater Conference Center Hotel, which boasts over thirty conference and meeting rooms totaling more than 550,000 square feet. In addition to hosting business functions, the facilities are frequently rented for banquets and weddings. Those whose travel plans are focused on leisure can select one of the Penn Stater's special packages, including several golf options. The hotel offers both a casual bar and grille and a slightly more upscale restaurant specializing in American cuisine.

THE PENN STATE Blue Band bursts out of the tunnel at 144 beats per minute. Band members slap your hands as they speed past you, leading the stadium in chanting, "Let's Go STATE!" Adrenaline rushes through your veins and you're not quite sure what's pounding louder, the driving beat of the bass drums or your heart that's about to explode from behind the PSU emblazoned on your chest. Very few drum majors have been entrusted to carry on the tradition of flipping for Penn State since it started in 1972, but it's now up to YOU to bring it to life at Beaver Stadium. Over the crowd's roar you hear the silks, majorettes, and the Blue Sapphire introduced over the loudspeaker to the electrified football fans. Slipping a whistle between your lips, you make your Acme Thunderer scream, signaling the band as they ripple downfield rank after rank. The drums play the roll-off and the band chants, "Out . . . Up!" as the instruments snap to attention

• • • • •

"Can You Tell Me How to Get . . . to Sesame Street?"

They may not have worked out the puppetry for Big Bird or composed Ernie's ode to his rubber duckie, but leaders in the fields of broadcasting, education, and government did indeed tell the nation how to get to "Sesame Street" when they met at the Nittany Lion Inn in 1952. Envisioning a television service that would be educational, not commercial, they laid plans that would eventually culminate in the creation of public television. Today, the Public Broadcasting Service includes Penn State's own WPSU-TV, which reaches more than 500,000 households in twenty-nine counties throughout central Pennsylvania and southern New York state. (Previously known as WPSX-TV, the station adopted the WPSU call letters in 2005.) WPSU broadcasts national PBS programs while producing hundreds of its own programs each year, including Small Ball: A Little League Story, Legendary Lighthouses, and plenty of Penn State sports—basketball, volleyball, gymnastics, and wrestling among them. In recent years, its Emmy-winning Center Court with Rene Portland has given viewers a unique behind-the-scenes look at Lady Lion basketball.

WPSU-FM, a National Public Radio and Public Radio International affiliate station, broadcasts to twelve counties in central and Northern Pennsylvania and has an audience of nearly half a million listeners. The station began in 1953 as a student-run radio station (called WDFM) and now, with more than 3,000 members, WPSU broadcasts national NPR productions such as Morning Edition, A Prairie Home Companion, and All Things Considered, as well as locally produced programs including The Folk Show and President Graham Spanier's To the Best of My Knowledge.

For years Penn State Public Broadcasting was located in the Wagner Building, but in 2005 it moved to new facilities—with state-of-the-art television and radio production studios—in Innovation Park.

• • • • •

Penn State Firsts, 1950–present

1951   Distinguished Alumnus Awards were created by trustees, and the first five awards were presented.

1956   The University Press was established with Louis H. Bell as first director; the first book, published in 1958, was E. J. Nichols's Toward Gettysburg.

1958   University trustees created the Penn State Woman of the Year Award, with Julia Gregg Brill as the first recipient.

1959   Charles W. Mann became the full-time curator of the library's rare book collection.

1960   Evan Pugh Research Professorships were created. Woldemar Weyl (ceramics) and Haskell Curry (mathematics) were the first recipients.

1971   The final issue of Faculty Bulletin was published, with the first issue of Intercom, its successor, published September 23.

1974   Helen I. Snyder, associate professor of educational psychology, was elected first woman chair of the Faculty Senate.

1978   Pam Davis, a psychology major from Philadelphia, was the first graduate of the Black Scholars program.

1981   Sara George, a sophomore economics major, became the first Penn State winner of a $20,000 Harry S. Truman Scholarship.

1983   The first Nuclear Magnetic Resonance (NMR) Imaging System in the Commonwealth was established at the Hershey Medical Center.

1985   Anthony Mandia, forty-four, of Philadelphia, was the first recipient of the Penn State Heart.

1989   Enrollment surpassed 70,000 students for first time.

1998   Tess Thompson was named Penn State's first Rhodes Scholar.

2000   College of Engineering ranked first nationally in number of B.S. degrees awarded (1,263).

2006   Nittany Lions won Orange Bowl 26-23 over Florida State in first triple overtime in Penn State history.

and the block starts a slow-motion high step. Making a final check of the chinstrap holding that large white hat on your head, you know there's no stopping now.

"Hail to the Lion" plays as you strut, breaking through the ranks into the open field. Your arms swing around as you plant your spikes into the soft, hallowed turf and vault into the air. Immediately, you tuck your chin to your chest, your knees hit your stomach, and you're upside down above the fifty-yard line in front of over 100,000 people. Opening up from the tuck, you see the blue sky above and you know you're about to hear an explosion. Sticking the landing, you spring high into the air and finish in a split. The cheer from the crowd is deafening. After you make your salute to the Press Box, a sense of relief flows over your body. You know you've done your part to ensure another Penn State victory.

—TOM ROBERTS, CLASS OF '94

SELECTED BIBLIOGRAPHY

Bezilla, Michael. *Penn State: An Illustrated History*. University Park: The Pennsylvania State University Press, 1985.

Esposito, Jackie R., and Steven L. Herb. *The Nittany Lion: An Illustrated Tale.* University Park, Pa.: The Pennsylvania State University Press, 1997.

Klauder, Charles Z., and Herbert C. Wise. *College Architecture in America and Its Part in the Development of the Campus.* New York: Charles Scribner's Sons, 1929.

Paris, Laura W. "Frederick L. Olds at the Early Buildings of Penn State." M.A. thesis, The Pennsylvania State University, 1998.

Pitluga, Kurt W. "Charles Z. Klauder at Penn State: The Image of the University." M.A. thesis, The Pennsylvania State University, 1990.

——. "The Collegiate Architecture of Charles Z. Klauder." Ph.D. diss., The Pennsylvania State University, 1994.

Prato, Louis, with Rob Falk. *The Penn State Football Encyclopedia.* Champaign, Ill.: Sports Publishing, 1998.

Range, Thomas E., II, and Sean Patrick Smith. *The Penn State Blue Band: A Century of Pride and Precision.* University Park, Pa.: The Pennsylvania State University Press, 1999.

Roberts, Len. "Pathways." From *The Silent Singer: New and Selected Poems.* Urbana: University of Illinois Press, 2001.

Sonenklar, Carol. *We Are a Strong, Articulate Voice: A History of Women at Penn State.* University Park, Pa.: The Pennsylvania State University Press, 2006.

Turner, Paul Venable. *Campus: An American Planning Tradition.* New York: The Architectural History Foundation; Cambridge, Mass.: MIT Press, 1984.

Zabel, Craig. *Palmer Museum of Art: A New Building by Charles W. Moore in Association with Arbonies King Vlock.* University Park: Palmer Museum of Art, The Pennsylvania State University, 1993.

At the Pennsylvania State University: Archives, pp. 2, 4, 5, 7, 9, 10, 13, 21 (right), 30, 32, 35, 37, 39, 44, 45, 46, 47, 48, 49, 52, 58, 60 (top right and bottom right), 63 (left), 65, 66, 67, 68, 69, 71 (right), 72, 79 (center and bottom), 87 (bottom), 88, 90 (left), 91, 92, 97, 99, 104, 106, 107, 108, 120, 121, 125, 126, 132; College of Arts and Architecture, 2004, photo Paul Kletchka, p. 78; College of Health and Human Development, p. 25; Bob Corman, Telecommunications and Networking Services, Special Projects Office, p. 79 (top); courtesy Department of Material Science and Engineering, p. 20; courtesy Earth and Mineral Sciences Museum, p. 21 (left); Frost Entomological Museum, p. 119; courtesy Greg Grieco, pp. iii©, x©, 22, 24, 30 (bottom), 33, 34, 36, 37, 38, 41, 53, 56, 59, 60 (left), 62, 63 (right), 64, 66, 73, 74, 77, 80, 81, 84 (top and left), 87 (top), 89, 90 (center), 96, 98, 101, 102, 104, 111, 114, 119, 122, 123, 124, 127, 130, 132 (bottom left); courtesy Cherene Holland, p. 28; William Hutton, University Libraries, p. 73; Chris Koleno, Department of Public Information, pp. 18, 40, 74, 81; Palmer Museum of Art, p. 83; University Publications, pp. 26, 29, 31, 70, 71 (left), 77, 93, 118; Devon Zahn, courtesy La Vie, pp. 23, 24, 129, 135. Roy Hilton's *The Miner*, c. 1936, p. 21 (left), Gift of Mr. and Mrs. Edmund G. Fox, class of 1925, Steidle Collection, College of Earth and Mineral Sciences Museum and Art Gallery, The Pennsylvania State University, University Park, Pennsylvania.

Bower Lewis Thrower Architects, p. 123; IKM Incorporated, Architects, p. 85.

Special thanks to Patty Mitchell, Laura Reed-Morrisson, and Mike Richards (who did the lion's share) as well as Brian Beer, Cherene Holland, Steve Kress, Jennifer Norton, and Steph Philip.

CREDITS